MARSHA TAYLOR

Persevere

Everyday Strength from the Book of Nehemiah

LUCIDBOOKS

Persevere
Everyday Strength from the Book of Nehemiah

Copyright © 2022 by Marsha Taylor

Published by Lucid Books in Houston, TX
www.lucidbooks.com

ISBN 978-1-63296-535-6 (paperback)
ISBN 978-1-63296-534-9 (ebook)

Special Sales: Most Lucid Books titles are available in special quantity discounts. Custom imprinting or
excerpting can also be done to fit special needs.
For standard bulk orders, go to www.lucidbooksbulk.com.
For specialty press or large orders, contact Lucid Books at info@lucidbooks.com.

Special Thanks

First and foremost, I am overwhelmed at the sacrifice of Jesus on my behalf, grateful for His blessing, and honored to serve Him as my Savior. This study has been difficult, and at times painful, to write. I am grateful for all He has taught me and the ways I have grown. I am different and I am better because He has lovingly shown me how to persevere.

I am so grateful for the encouragement of the following friends and family who have listened to me, challenged me, and supported me in this endeavor:

- To my husband, David – you are my rock, my support, and my best friend. I am so thankful for you. Thank you for your loving me so well!

- To Caroline and Catherine & Will – I am truly blessed by being your mom & mom-in-law. You bring so much joy to my life.

- To Melissa, Denise, Karen, Jamie, Jill, Janie & Patt – thank you for the hours you spent in the focus group, reading and working through each lesson and offering sound advice and gentle correction. Your support and encouragement have been invaluable.

- To Maureen – thank you for your constant support, listening ear, sound advice, and help in persevering through the writing process.

Table of Contents

Purpose

How "Persevere" is Designed

Persevere is designed for daily study in God's Word. Each lesson covers a specific passage of scripture from Nehemiah and divides the focal passage into five days of study. Ideally, you should complete one lesson per week. My desire is for you to search your Bible to find deeper meaning and personal application of the truths. The questions are designed for you to answer with your own thoughts and ideas from the scripture and not simply write the verse verbatim from your Bible.

I have written the study in a conversational style, which may be different than other studies you have done. I want each reader and student to feel they have someone by their side as they are studying. If you are a person who likes to read the scripture chapters in order, please know that we will skip around some since the chapters are organized by topic rather than verse order, but we will study all of Nehemiah.

Each day's lesson in the workbook is estimated to take 20–40 minutes, and the entire lesson should take 1–2 hours. The questions use the English Standard Version (ESV) of the Bible unless designated otherwise. If you are using another version and do not understand a question or the answer, please check the ESV for clarity.

I believe that the time you spend in God's Word will be extremely beneficial. **Hebrews 4:12** tells us that His Word is living and active, so each time you look at scripture, God is going to speak to your heart to bring you encouragement, correction, or instruction. Oh, friend, that can be a specific word about something He wants to do or change in your life, something about the situation or circumstances you are facing, something about His character and His love for you, or something altogether new. Whatever He wants to say, it is thrilling to hear the very words of God speaking to your soul.

So, dig in! Enjoy the depth of each verse you look up. My desire in writing this study is to take you into the Old and New Testaments to see for yourself that God is the same yesterday, today, and forever and to learn how all scripture works together beautifully to glorify God and point us to His Son, Jesus.

Do your best to complete the lessons without consulting a commentary for assistance. Commentaries can be excellent tools for additional study, but it is more meaningful when you find the answer in His Word alone. Pray, and ask God to help you find the answer to a question you are struggling with or is challenging to you.

God wants you to learn from Him and His Word, and it is thrilling when He teaches you.

Resources

To enhance your study, there are teaching videos that accompany each week's lesson. If you are able to work through this book in a group setting with your friends or at your church, discussion questions are also available.

Both resources can be downloaded at www.freshsurrender.org.

For Leaders

If you are interested in leading a group in your home, community, or church, please visit www.freshsurrender.org for additional materials to download free of charge.

Small group discussion questions, listening guides to accompany the video teaching, and administrative materials to help facilitate a class are also available on the website.

If you are interested in teaching the material rather than using the video content and facilitating a group, please know that is thrilling to me. I am praying that teachers will find the workbook content complementary to their teaching.

Introduction

Don't we all wish our lives could be filled with happiness and good things without pain and disappointment? We long for our days to be easy, our relationships to be simple, and our spiritual journey to bring complete satisfaction. Oh, that we could grow in our faith and maturity without the hard times! But just as there are seasons in nature, our lives are filled with different seasons. Nature is cyclical. There are the beautiful seasons of spring and summer when flowers bloom, the grass is green, the birds chirp, and cool water begs us to dive in for a nice swim. There are also the seasons of fall and winter when leaves die on their branches, flowers cease blooming, and cold and darkness seem to come with a vengeance.

Just as there are seasons in nature, there are also seasons in our lives. Some seasons bring joy and delight while others are painful and difficult. When we are in the midst of challenging times, it can seem hard to just get through the day. In order to endure the seasons, we need to be prepared and know how to be strengthened so we can continue, solid in our faith. We must be prepared to persevere because if we are not experiencing difficulty now, we are sure to face some degree of discouraging circumstances, challenging relationships, or defeating thoughts in the future.

We will have seasons of hurt, challenge, and pain, but they do not have to defeat us. That is why I love the book of Nehemiah. Through the events in the book of Nehemiah, we can find the courage to keep going, persevere in our trials, and emerge from difficult times more in love with Jesus, God's Word, and the people around us.

To have a better understanding of the book of Nehemiah, we must have a very general knowledge of biblical history up to the time of Nehemiah. We do not need to go back to the beginning of God's creation of the world and the fall of Adam and Eve, but let's begin our historical look with Abram.

Abram and His Family—The Promise

In the 12th chapter of Genesis, Abram is called by God out of his country, Ur, to a land God promised to show him. By faith, Abram obeys God and sets out with his wife, his father, his nephew, and his nephew's family, not knowing where they are going but trusting that God will show them where to go. In **Genesis 15**, God makes a covenant with Abram, again promising to give him a land. In addition, God changes his name to Abraham and tells him He has chosen his family line to bring forth the Messiah and that all nations will be blessed through Abraham. Pretty big promise! And through this promise, we see God's love for all nations.

The book of Genesis continues with the story of Abraham's family. As Abraham's story unfolds, God gives him a twofold promise: (1) a land the Jewish nation will call their own and (2) a Savior, the promised Messiah, Who will come from Abraham's family line. This promised blessing follows through Abraham's son Isaac and Isaac's son Jacob.

The final stories in Genesis are of Jacob and his 12 sons, the most well-known being Joseph who was sold into slavery by his brothers and taken to Egypt. While there, Joseph wins the favor of Pharaoh by interpreting his dreams. Through God's revelation, Joseph is also forewarned of a coming famine. With Pharaoh's authority, Joseph stockpiles grain so the people in the country will not go hungry. The book of Genesis ends with a famine and Jacob and his sons traveling to Egypt for food.

> Have you wondered how the Israelites got their name? The Bible tells of a time when Jacob wrestled all night with a "man" who, once the sun came up, identified Himself as God. Following this, God changes Jacob's name to "Israel." All those born to Jacob (Israel) and the following generations have been referred to as "Israelites," denoting they are part of Israel's family.

Deliverance from Exile—Moses and Joshua

As Exodus begins, we see that the previous generation has died, and the descendants of Abraham and Jacob have multiplied to a great number in Egypt. Fearing their number, the Pharaoh of Egypt decides to enslave the Israelites and oppress them greatly until God raises up a leader—a man named Moses—to bring them out of captivity. The Israelites spend 430 years in captivity in Egypt before God delivers them.

While Moses successfully leads the Israelites' exit from Egypt, the Israelites fall into sin. As punishment, God forces them to wander in the wilderness for 40 years, as told in the books of Exodus and Deuteronomy, which ends with the death of Moses.

Deuteronomy is also the end of the books of the Law, comprised of the first five books of the Old Testament—Genesis, Exodus, Leviticus, Numbers, and Deuteronomy. These five books are also known as the Torah. They are designed by God to show us the image of perfection, to show how far we have fallen from that standard, and to show us our desperate need for God.

Following the death of Moses, Joshua takes over and finally leads God's chosen people into the Promised Land of Canaan. At that point, the land is divided according to the sons of Israel (Jacob), giving the descendants of each son a dispensation of land. These groups are known as the tribes of Israel. God appoints men and women called judges to govern the people of the land.

A Cry for a King and the Fall Back into Captivity

All seems great, right? Wrong. Even though God tells Joshua and the Israelites to drive out all the foreign inhabitants of the Promised Land, they did not obey. As they look around at other nations, they desire to be ruled as other countries are—by a king. They ask and beg God to give them a king to rule them rather than the judges.

So, God gives them what they ask for, and Saul is anointed as the first king of Israel. However, Saul does not obey God, and God rejects him as king. God then chooses David, a young shepherd boy, who eventually replaces Saul after many years of waiting. Following David as king is David's son Solomon, whose reign begins in the book of 1 Kings. At the death of King Solomon in 931 BC, Israel is split into two parts—the Northern Kingdom (referred to as Israel and comprised of 10 tribes) and the Southern Kingdom (referred to as Judah and comprised of two tribes).

These kingdoms begin to fall away, swayed by the negative influences around them, and begin worshipping other gods. In 722 BC, the Northern Kingdom falls into Assyrian captivity, never to be united again. The Southern Kingdom falls into Babylonian captivity in 587 BC, but they remained intact and united.

The Return to Jerusalem

When Babylon is invaded by the Medes and Persians in 539 BC, the Medes allow the exiles of the Southern Kingdom to return to Jerusalem. Zerubbabel leads approximately 50,000 people out of Babylon, and they begin rebuilding the temple in Jerusalem. However, by 450 BC, this remnant falls into temptation and fear because there is no wall around the city for protection to keep them safe from outside influences and threats.

Ezra, who is a priest, is called by God to lead a second group of exiles back to Jerusalem. This second group is much smaller in number (about 2,000) than the group Zerubbabel led, and Ezra's call for repentance in the city is effective. Most of the Israelites in Jerusalem return to worshiping God. That brings us to 444 BC and the first chapter of Nehemiah.

The Book of Nehemiah

It is unclear who penned the book of Nehemiah, but scholars believe it was most likely Nehemiah or Ezra who copied the information from Nehemiah's journals. Either way, the books of Ezra and Nehemiah are so similar in layout that many believed the same person wrote them. Both Ezra and Nehemiah have very important jobs in the rebuilding of Jerusalem. Ezra is the priest responsible for the spiritual well-being of the people and rebuilding the temple. Nehemiah is a layman, responsible for rebuilding the wall around the city.

Before being tasked with rebuilding the wall around Jerusalem, Nehemiah was the cupbearer to the King of Persia. It was a position of great responsibility and privilege. As a cupbearer, Nehemiah tested the king's wine at every meal to make sure it was not poisoned. As a man who stood that close to the king, Nehemiah had to be cultured, knowledgeable of court procedures, handsome, and able to converse with and advise the king. Overall, the cupbearer was a man of great influence.

God had a work for Nehemiah to do and placed him in the king's palace for a reason. Nehemiah was in a position where he could influence the King of Persia to give the permission and resources required to accomplish the task of building a wall around Jerusalem. When God wants to accomplish a work, he always prepares His workers and places them in the right place at the right time. It was true for Nehemiah and it is true for us today.

A Word of Encouragement to Begin

As we begin our study, I believe we are going to learn so much from Nehemiah! We will see that we should have a passionate concern for our fellow brothers and sisters in Christ. We will see the need to have deep prayer lives that touch the heart of God. We will watch Nehemiah persevere and see his obedient spirit submit to God's will. We will see what effective Christian leadership looks like and learn the importance of building healthy boundaries in our lives so we can keep our lives pure and resist the evil influences that exist in our world.

Approximate Timeline of Old Testament History

2200 BC   The call of Abraham

1445 BC   The Exodus

1406 BC   Inhabiting the Promised Land of Canaan

1350 BC   First king of Israel anointed

931 BC   Israel divided into two kingdoms—the Northern Kingdom (Israel) and the Southern Kingdom (Judah)
For our study, we will concentrate on Judah, which is where Jerusalem was located.

587/86 BC   King Nebuchadnezzar of Babylon invades Judah; takes Jews to Babylon and into captivity

539 BC   King Cyrus of Persia conquers Babylon

537 BC   Zerubbabel returns with the first group of exiles

536 BC   Work on the temple begins

530 BC   Work on the temple ceases under Persian King Cambyses

520 BC   Under King Darius II, work on the temple begins again

516 BC   The temple is completed

471 BC   Events of the Book of Esther under King Xerxes I (Ahasuerus)

458 BC   Ezra returns with the second group of exiles

444 BC   The Book of Nehemiah begins under King Artaxerxes

444 BC   Nehemiah returns with the third group of exiles

Tina - coworker of Samantha

Dustin - coworker of Ernest

Bailey Morrison - graduating from college

LESSON ONE

Get On Your Knees

— NEHEMIAH 1:1-11 —

As we begin our study, it is important to remember that Nehemiah was a man of excellence. To be in the position of the cupbearer to the king, he must have been well-educated, cultured, and well-spoken. In terms of being a servant of God, though, he was a typical, regular person. He was not called to be a prophet or a priest. He was just an ordinary man going about his ordinary business when he received news concerning his fellow Jewish countrymen struggling in Jerusalem. His heart was tender – tender toward other people and tender toward their struggles.

As we look at the characteristics we need to persevere, the first thing we see in Nehemiah is that he saw the needs and concerns of other people and immediately took his concern to the Lord. He knew that God would provide the answers. When confronted with the problem, Nehemiah interceded for the needs of others.

I think we often get our eyes on ourselves and neglect to see the needs of others, losing concern for what is happening in the world around us. After all, we have responsibilities in our jobs, our families, our volunteer activities, our civic involvements, our social engagements, and our churches and Bible study activity. There are so many things to do . . . and so little time, right?

But for Nehemiah, his concern for others was evident. He asked for a report on his kinsmen. I am sure he was busy with his own affairs, but he cared enough to ask about them. In our own busyness of life, sometimes we see the needs and hurts in others around us, but all too often we choose to not take the time to ask about what we see when we notice others hurting.

More often than we would like to admit, we prefer not to ask others about their circumstances or hurts because with the knowledge of need comes responsibility. Once we are aware of someone in need, aren't we in some way responsible to do something to help? We might need to take them a meal, drive them to an appointment, watch their children, lend a hand, or, most importantly, pray for them. A true concern for others takes time, and sadly, it is time that we often feel we do not have to give.

Nehemiah genuinely cared and wanted to hear how his kinsmen were doing. He was willing to invest his time, and he understood that only by the power of God would the situation change for his fellow countrymen. And so, he prayed.

DAY 1
— THE FALL - TAKEN CAPTIVE —

When beginning to study a book in the Bible, it is important to understand the historical context in which the book is written. For the first two days of our study, we will dive into the history behind Nehemiah and other books in the Old Testament that will help us understand Nehemiah's heart and concern. This concern is what drives Nehemiah to his knees.

1 To understand how Nehemiah came to live in Babylon, we need to go back to the book of **2 Kings**. According to **2 Kings 24:8–9**, who was the king of Judah, and what do you learn about his actions in the sight of God?

Jehoiachin = evil in the sight of God

2 Read the account of the siege of Jerusalem in **2 Kings 24:10–17**.

Who came against Jerusalem in **verses 10–11**?

Neb of Babylon

How did the king respond to the attack according to **verse 12**?

surrendered

What happened to the treasures of the house of the Lord (the temple) and the house of the king? (See **verse 13**)

Neb carried away + stripped away

Who was taken to Babylon in **verses 14–17**? Write as many details as you can about these verses.

_____

_____

_____

_____

_____

_____

According to **verse 14**, who remained in Jerusalem?

_____

_____

_____

_____

3 Following the siege, Nebuchadnezzar established Jehoiachin's uncle as king of Judah, who not only continued doing evil in God's sight but also rebelled against Nebuchadnezzar. What happened in **2 Kings 25:1**?

_____

_____

_____

_____

4 What happened in the following verses?

2 Kings 25:9

_____

_____

_____

2 Kings 25:10

_____

_____

_____

2 Kings 25:13–15

_____

_____

_____

5

We end today with the Israelites in captivity in Babylon. Have you ever been there—in some sort of captivity? Maybe it wasn't a literal prison, but we have all been in dark places where there seems to be little hope. Maybe you are held captive by your past. Maybe your thoughts and fears lock you in a prison at times. Oh, friend, there is hope in Jesus and His power to release you from captivity. **Isaiah 61:1–3** is a prophetic word spoken before it came to be. It talks about Jesus Christ. What does this verse say Jesus came to earth to do? How would you like to thank Jesus for His work to bring you into freedom?

_____

_____

_____

_____

DAY 2
— THE ROAD TO RETURN —

Today we will continue looking at the history leading up to Nehemiah's day. Approximately 60 years have passed since the Jews were carried off into captivity in Babylon. During that time, the Persian king Cyrus conquers Babylon, thus destroying the Babylonian Empire as the Persian Empire rises to power. It is important to note that the Jewish captives are located in the same place. The name has just changed to reflect the ruling power. We are also going to see several kings come to power in these years, Cyrus will lose his kingdom to Darius, followed by Cambyses (or Artaxerxes), then another king named Darius, then Xerxes, and finally a completely different Artaxerxes. Do not worry too much about their names. Just understand that several different men seem to have the same name.

Refer to the timeline in the Introduction if you are confused.

1

What does Cyrus, King of Persia, declare in **Ezra 1:1–4**?

_____

_____

_____

_____

2 The people who were determined to return to Jerusalem were led by Zerubbabel. How many returned in this first group according to **Ezra 2:64**?

_____

_____

_____

3 As the people begin rebuilding the temple of God in Jerusalem, what happens according to **Ezra 4:4–5**?

_____

_____

_____

4 These same discouragers send a letter to the king. What is the king's response to this news according to **Ezra 4:21**, and what is the result in **Ezra 4:24**?

_____

_____

_____

Work ceases for 10 years until King Darius (the second one by the same name) issues yet another decree to allow work on the temple to resume, and the work on the temple is finally complete.

5 Another 59 years pass before Ezra, a Jewish priest, is allowed to return to Jerusalem. According to **Ezra 7:15–20**, what does Ezra take back with him?

_____

_____

_____

_____

_____

_____

6 What do you learn about the house of the Lord (the temple) from **2 Chronicles 2:4–5**?

_____

_____

_____

Now our stage is set. An additional 12–14 years will pass until our story continues with God's servant Nehemiah.

DAY 3
— READ *NEHEMIAH 1:1-4* —

1 As we begin the first chapter of Nehemiah, it has been approximately 100 years since Zerubbabel took the first group of Jews back to Jerusalem to rebuild the city following their exile in Babylon. When Nehemiah's brother returns to Susa from Jerusalem, Nehemiah asks about the status of those in Jerusalem and the city. What does Hanani report according to **verse 3**?

_____

_____

_____

_____

2 What is Nehemiah's response to the news according to **verse 4**?

_____

_____

_____

3 All too often in our society we see tears as a sign of weakness and try not to let others see when our hearts are downcast. What do the following verses say about our tears and weeping?

Psalm 56:8

_____ You keep track of all tears _____

_____

_____

Psalm 126:5

_____ Those who plant in tears will _____
_____ harvest with shouts of joy. _____

_____

Ecclesiastes 3:1, 4

_____

_____

_____

Romans 12:15

_____

_____

_____

4 The verses below speak about what we will experience in eternity. What do they tell us that God will do with our tears once and for all in our heavenly home?

Isaiah 25:8

_____

_____

_____

Revelation 7:17

_____

_____

_____

5 Nehemiah is moved to tears since his heart is burdened by the needs of others. In our own lives, there are hurting people around us. Are you willing to listen to them and cry with them over their sorrows? Has God brought someone to your mind that you need to pray for? Why not encourage them with a phone call, a note, or a visit to offer them a shoulder to cry on and a friend to cry with? In the space below, write the name of a person God brings to your mind and any encouragement you find during the week as you follow through with contacting them.

_____

_____

_____

_____

_____

_____

_____

DAY 4
— READ *NEHEMIAH 1:5-7* —

Life can sometimes throw us some challenging curves. When a difficult situation arises in your life or you hear about a friend in need, what is your first response? Is it to pick up the phone to chat with a friend, seek their advice, and discuss what is going on? Or is your first response to take your need to God in prayer? In the book of Nehemiah, there are 12 instances of prayer, so it seems that prayer was of vital importance to Nehemiah. When things are difficult in our lives or the lives of others, we should always take our needs to God first. Prayer should be our priority.

Nehemiah begins his prayer by focusing on God. Once confronted with the holiness of God, he becomes aware of his own sin. This is the first step in approaching God with our requests—offering our adoration to Him as our almighty, powerful God and then confessing our sin and our need for Him and His forgiveness.

→ focus on God
→ God is Holy
→ I am sinful
— confession
— our need for Him
— our need for forgiveness

1   Nehemiah begins his prayer by reverently focusing on the characteristics of Almighty God. What does he say in **verse 5**?

great, awesome, unfailing love,

_____

_____

_____

_____

2   What are some other attributes or characteristics of God you see in the following verses?

Deuteronomy 7:9

faithful, unfailing love

God is God

_____

Deuteronomy 32:4

the rock, deeds are perfect
does no wrong (just & fair faithful)

Romans 11:33

riches, wisdom, knowledge
impossible for us to discern Him

In **verses 6–7**, Nehemiah recognizes his unworthiness and sin and immediately confesses his transgressions to God. How do the verses below speak of confessing our own sins to God?

Psalm 32:1–5

freedom in confession

Psalm 38:18

confession

Psalm 51:2–4

sin haunts us
cleanse me from my sin.

What do you learn from the following verses about God's forgiveness?

2 Chronicles 7:14

humble, pray, seek God, repent,

Psalm 51:7–10

we need to be transformed

Psalm 103:12

sin is forgiven when taken to the Lord. East to the West

1 John 1:9

confession leads to forgiveness

5 What did God show you in your study today? Did you see a new beauty in Him that you want to praise Him for? Are you reminded of a sin you need to confess? Why not write a prayer to Him in adoration for all He is, confess your sin to Him, and thank Him for His complete forgiveness of all your transgressions?

confession - aknowledging your sinfulness
giving into pride
- aligning your heart with God
- God already knows of our sin,
- cleansing

DAY 5

— READ *NEHEMIAH 1:8-11* —

"There is too much working before men and too little waiting before God."[1]

—Alan Redpath

1

In **verses 8–9**, Nehemiah reminds God of the promises He made to the Israelites. What does Nehemiah say to God in his prayer in **verse 10**?

_____

_____

_____

_____

2

Nehemiah boldly asks God to grant him success and mercy before man (the king). What do the following verses say about bringing your requests to God?

Psalm 62:5–8

*Pour out your heart to Him
God is our refuge.*

Hebrews 4:16

Come boldly to the throne

Philippians 4:6

*Don't worry
Pray about everything*

3 What do the following verses say about God's response to our prayers?

Psalm 4:3

_____

_____

_____

Matthew 7:7–11

Ask God

Seek Him

Philippians 4:19

He will supply our

needs

4 While we should approach God's throne with boldness in our request, He may not always answer us in the way we expect or in the time frame we want. What do the following verses say about God's answers?

Psalm 69:13

answer with sure salvation

_____

_____

Proverbs 3:5–6

Trust in the Lord

He will direct your path

Proverbs 16:9

Make plans

Lord determines our steps

Isaiah 55:8–9

My thoughts & ways are

nothing like Gods

5 Nehemiah boldly asks God for what he wants. He has acknowledged God's greatness, recognized and repented over his own sin, and poured out his heart before the Lord. What need has been on your heart recently that you would like to pour out before God in boldness?

_____

_____

_____

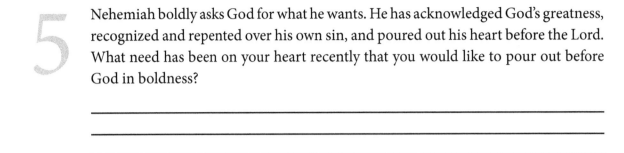

Concluding Thoughts

Someone delivered some hard news to me yesterday. It seemed like things were going well, and then suddenly things were said in passing that hit me like a punch in the gut. The news hurt me to the core, brought discouragement, and made me question my place in service and my calling. Tears flowed down my cheeks as I questioned everything that seemed so clear just hours before.

I have written most of this lesson with tears in my eyes. Do I understand everything God is doing? No. Do I know how He is going to intervene in my circumstances? No. How I need the encouragement found in His Word! I am still confused and hurt, but just like Nehemiah, my calling is to persevere. I am not sure what to do, but I know I must be obedient to His calling for me, and I am setting my mind to take the next step. Do I know where I am headed? No, but I am surrendered to Him and willing to follow Him whenever He makes it clear.

With many tears, I have poured out my heart before Him, and I know He has heard my cry. I love knowing that He has stored my tears in His bottle (**Psalm 56:8**). I feel so loved knowing that my God is so close to me during this time—close enough to have His hand on my cheek as He catches each tear, teardrops that are so precious to Him that He saves them.

I have needed my friends' prayers and support this week. Just like Nehemiah heard the news of his countrymen and went to God on their behalf, I have needed my friends to intercede for me, lift me up, and ask God to bring restoration to my soul. Friends have wept with me and prayed for me, and I am so grateful. I have needed those who are willing to ask how I am and ready to carry my burden before the Lord on my behalf.

I have also wept bitterly and poured out my heart before God in my own prayers. I think we all need to learn to take our time with God and pour out our hearts before Him. Our lives are often filled with hurts and disappointments that we try to bear ourselves. Nehemiah could not have borne the pain he felt all alone, so he wept and mourned and poured out his heart before God. How often are we afraid to do that because we think we will shock God or anger Him with the depth of our emotions? We will not. He already knows it; He knows everything about us.

In **Psalm 62:8** we are told, "Trust in Him at all times, O people. Pour out your heart before Him. God is a safe place for us." (NLT) You can trust God with your heart no matter how broken you are. He has the power to heal and put us back together.

Tell Him about your hurt, your disappointment, your anger. Maybe you even need to tattle on someone who has devastated you. It is important to take the time to pour yourself out before your Heavenly Father and let Him heal your wounds and bind up your broken heart.

Maybe you need to set aside time to pray and get your heart right before Him. Do you need to confess the areas of your life where you have allowed sin to take hold of you? Do you need to get back into the right relationship with Him? When we allow sin to linger in our lives, we build a wall between us and our Heavenly Father, and it becomes difficult for us to come to Him with a clear conscience.

Oh, friend, we need to be willing to wait for God to open doors before we try to barge through them. During those times of waiting, God is teaching us. He is molding our character and preparing us for what is ahead. Our job is to persevere in prayer and be ready to go when He says "now."

Is there something you have been waiting on God to answer? How prepared are you if He answers your prayer today?

Additional Notes

_____

_____

_____

_____

_____

_____

_____

LESSON TWO

Don't Be Afraid To Act

— NEHEMIAH 2:1-18 —

Nehemiah is burdened for his countrymen and his homeland. He has prayed for God's direction and boldly asked God for answers, and yet four months have passed between Chapter 1 and Chapter 2. The worry and concern Nehemiah has for those in Jerusalem is now affecting his job, and the king confronts Nehemiah about his demeanor.

In his position as the king's cupbearer, Nehemiah needs to be winsome as well as alert in the king's presence since he is (in a way) the king's bodyguard. Nehemiah's emotional distress could have affected his duties. Any servant of the king was required to not show any sadness in the king's presence. Nehemiah cannot contain his despondency any longer, and it is evident to the king. If the king feels this display is treasonous or if he is displeased, Nehemiah could lose his position or his life.

No wonder Nehemiah utters a quick prayer when asked why he is downcast. He has been waiting for God to answer his prayer for four months, and now he has the opportunity to ask the king for help, not knowing how he will respond. So Nehemiah, with great boldness, shares his heart with the king and walks away from the conversation with the king's favor and more.

"Real prayer keeps your heart and your head in balance so your burden doesn't make you impatient to run ahead of the Lord and ruin everything."[2]

—Warren Wiersbe

DAY 1

— READ NEHEMIAH 2:1-4 —

1   Read **Nehemiah 2:1-3**. What does the king notice about Nehemiah? How does Nehemiah respond to the king's question?

_____

_____

_____

_____

2   Nehemiah has been praying about the situation in Jerusalem for months. He does not run ahead of the Lord or try to solve the situation on his own. God is working behind the scenes and opens the door at this moment so Nehemiah can approach the king. What do the following verses say about waiting on the Lord?

Isaiah 64:4

_____

_____

_____

_____

Psalm 27:14

_____

_____

_____

_____

Psalm 37:5, 7

_____

_____

_____

_____

3 How do the following verses encourage you about God's faithfulness and ability to answer prayer?

Psalm 17:6

_____

_____

_____

Psalm 38:15

_____

_____

_____

Psalm 69:13

_____

_____

_____

Zechariah 13:9b

_____

_____

_____

4 Finally, Nehemiah is asked to present his request before the king, and he takes a moment before he answers. What does he do in the moment following the king's question according to **Nehemiah 2:4**?

_____

_____

_____

_____

5 As difficult as it is, at times we must wait on God to bring answers to our prayers and relief to our distraught hearts. Read **Isaiah 40:31**. What encouragement do you draw from this verse?

_____

_____

_____

_____

DAY 2

— READ *NEHEMIAH 2:5–8* —

Nehemiah knows God is powerful and can do all things, and he is not afraid to be used by God in any way God sees fit. His attitude is like that of the prophet Isaiah who heard God calling him and answered by saying, "Here am I. Send me!" (**Isaiah 6:8**). Nehemiah is ready to be used by God for His purposes, and it is through his prayer life that God provides clarity and a vision of what needs to be done. When the time comes, Nehemiah stepped out in faith, ready to see God move.

1 Read **Nehemiah 2:5–8.** According to verses 5, 7, and 8, what does Nehemiah ask the king for? What is the king's response?

_____

_____

_____

2 In **Nehemiah 2:8**, Nehemiah testifies that the good hand of God is upon him. What do the following verses say about obtaining the favor of God?

Psalm 5:11–12

_____

_____

_____

Psalm 84:11

_____

_____

_____

Proverbs 3:3–6

_____

_____

_____

3 There are times when God answers our prayers with a different answer than we were hoping to receive. In **Psalm 84:11**, we saw that God does not withhold any good thing from us. That means that if He has not given you something you desire, He has determined it is not a good thing for you. Can you recall a time when you asked God for something and He said no, only later to realize how gracious God was in not giving you what you wanted? Have you thanked Him for His protection?

_____

_____

_____

4 Nehemiah is obedient to God and asks the king for his permission to go to Jerusalem to repair the wall around the city. What do the following verses say about obeying God?

John 14:15

_____

_____

_____

1 John 2:3–4

_____

_____

_____

1 John 5:2–3

_____

_____

_____

5 When we are obedient to God's Word, He can show His favor in our lives. While our obedience can result in His blessing, there is nothing we can do to earn God's favor and bring about our own salvation. Salvation is a gift solely of His grace. How is this expressed in **Ephesians 2:8–9**?

_____

_____

_____

_____

_____

DAY 3
— READ *NEHEMIAH 2:9* —

1 In yesterday's lesson, we looked at the supplies Nehemiah received in **Nehemiah 2:7–8**. According to **Nehemiah 2:9**, what additional support does the king provide Nehemiah?

_____

_____

_____

_____

_____

_____

_____

2 Our King of kings also gives to His children in abundance. What do you learn in the following verses?

Luke 6:38

_____

_____

_____

Ephesians 3:20–21

_____

_____

_____

Philippians 4:19

_____

_____

_____

3   Nehemiah is a great leader who steps out in faith and obedience when God called. Another great leader in the Old Testament is Joshua who became the leader of the Israelites after Moses' death. What do you learn from **Joshua 1:7–8** that will encourage you to step out in faith and obedience to something God is asking of you?

_____

_____

_____

_____

4   Approximately 14 years before Nehemiah, Ezra led a group of exiles out of Babylon and back to Jerusalem. This was the group of people Nehemiah is so concerned about. Read **Ezra 8:21–23**, and record what you learn about how the exiles were protected on their journey.

_____

_____

_____

5   I do not believe that Ezra was disobedient in not asking for protection from the king, and I am encouraged to know that as he stepped out in faith to restore the temple in Jerusalem and be the religious leader for the Israelites, God was their protection. While both Ezra and Nehemiah were tasked with rebuilding the city of Jerusalem, their calling was different. Ezra was a priest, and Nehemiah was a layman. I love seeing God's provision for Nehemiah on his journey, but I especially like the thought that the king did not allow Nehemiah to go on his way unprotected. He sent an army with him. What do you learn about the Lord's protection from the following verses?

Psalm 91:4

_____

_____

_____

Psalm 91:14–15

_____

_____

_____

DAY 4

— READ *NEHEMIAH 2:5-8* —

The journey to Jerusalem takes Nehemiah and his companions two months. Since first hearing of the difficult circumstances his countrymen are facing in Jerusalem, it has been six long months. He finally arrives in Jerusalem. Can you even imagine what his emotions were like? He was finally able to see the wall for himself, knowing he was sent by God to make a difference. Today we will focus on Nehemiah's first steps into the city.

1   We learn that Nehemiah arrives in Jerusalem. After he is there three days, what does he do, according to **Nehemiah 2:12–16**?

_____

_____

_____

_____

_____

2   Just as Nehemiah waited on the Lord to bring about the answer to his prayer, we see that he waits to disclose the plans God has given him to rebuild the wall around Jerusalem. He carefully takes in all the information about the condition of the wall and the gates of the city. What do you learn about wise planning before you act from the following verses?

Psalm 37:23

_____

_____

_____

Proverbs 16:3

_____

_____

_____

James 4:13–15

_____

_____

_____

3 There is also much wisdom in keeping silent and waiting for God's timing before speaking. Read **Psalm 62:5–8**, and record any encouragement you see in waiting on Him.

_____

_____

_____

_____

4 As we prepare to step out in faith, it is important to act according to God's plan and not our own. How does **Isaiah 55:8–9** encourage you to seek God's ways above all?

_____

_____

_____

_____

5 When difficulties come our way, it is so easy to react emotionally in both our speech and our actions and rush ahead of the Lord in our own planning. What have you learned today about slowing down and making sure your words and plans are of the Lord?

_____

_____

_____

_____

DAY 5

— READ *NEHEMIAH 2:17-20* —

The scene is set. We have seen Nehemiah enter Jerusalem bearing the authority of the king to continue rebuilding the city. He is carrying all the supplies to complete the work, and the king's military is there to protect him. He has rested from his journey, surveyed the ruins of the city and its gates, and determined what needs to be done. Now it is time to gather the workers and encourage them to join him in the task. Can you imagine how those weary inhabitants of Jerusalem must have felt? I am sure there was a fresh sense of hope that came into Jerusalem when Nehemiah entered the city and an excitement that God was at work. Now, after days of waiting, it is time for the work to begin.

1   Read **Nehemiah 2:17–18**. What does Nehemiah tell the people in Jerusalem, and what positive words of encouragement do you see?

_____

_____

_____

_____

_____

2   What encouragement do you see in the following verses?

Isaiah 35:3–4

_____

_____

_____

Isaiah 41:10

_____

_____

_____

Philippians 4:13

_____

_____

_____

3

We began our study this week by looking at Nehemiah's response to hearing of the need of his countrymen in Jerusalem. What do you learn about responding to the needs of others in the following verses?

Romans 12:13–15

_____

_____

_____

Galatians 6:2

_____

_____

_____

James 5:16

_____

_____

_____

4

Nehemiah has great concern for others, and his immediate action is to take that need before God in prayer. Nehemiah knows that God can answer his prayer and meet the needs of those suffering in Jerusalem. He is confident that God will answer. God's power is the same today as it was in Nehemiah's day. What burdens do you have for yourself or others that you want to commit to Him in prayer?

_____

_____

_____

_____

_____

_____

_____

Concluding Thoughts

Here am I, send me
Isaiah
6:8

When we are in difficult circumstances, it is easy to become paralyzed in our own emotions and do absolutely nothing. Fear can overtake us, and stepping out to make a change or confront a situation can seem completely overwhelming.

In addition, if we are not careful, our emotions can run away with us, leading us to act in anger, frustration, fear, or in our own wisdom to try to solve a situation in our own way. Likewise, how often do we let our emotions take control and suddenly hear ourselves talking way too much? Words we are not intending to say somehow slip out through our lips.

Nehemiah is a great reminder of stepping out in faith. First, we must know we have prayed for His wisdom and His timing. We must be prepared by reading His Word and committing our ways to Him. And when He says go, we can take that step of faith without fear. We must have a faith that is completely confident in God—that He is in control and that He is sovereign. We act according to His will and in His wisdom. Martin Luther said, "Faith is a living, daring confidence in God's grace. It is so sure and certain that a man could stake his life on it a thousand times." Nehemiah had that kind of faith.

When God puts something on our minds, how often do we think He is supposed to immediately open all the doors to get the task accomplished? And when we do not see the immediate answer, we bang on that door and try to open it ourselves until we are exhausted. Know this—God uses time. He is taking time to teach us, time to mold our character and time to prepare us for what is ahead. If it is a door God plans for you to walk through, you will never have to force it open. He will do it according to His timing.

Be willing to wait for God to open doors before you try to barge through them. Persevere in prayer, and be ready to go when He says now. And once God says go, know that you have the full authority of the throne of God with you. You may proceed with full confidence that the unseen but very real power of God is backing you up.

"We are prepared to serve the Lord only by sacrifice. We are fit for the work of God only when we have wept over it, prayed about it, and then we are enabled by Him to tackle the job that needs to be done. May God give to us hearts that bleed, eyes that are wide open to see, minds that are clear to interpret God's purpose, wills that are obedient, and a determination that is utterly unflinching as we set about the tasks He would have us do."[3]

—Alan Redpath

Additional Notes

_____
_____
_____
_____
_____
_____
_____
_____
_____
_____
_____
_____
_____
_____
_____
_____

LESSON THREE

Know Your Enemy

— NEHEMIAH 2:19–20, 4:1–22, 6:1–14 —

Nehemiah has assessed the land and determined the work that needs to be done. He is ready to get to the business of restoring Jerusalem's wall to protect the city and the temple of God. And just when it seems like everything is going well, Scripture records a disparaging "but." The enemy rears his ugly head. It is the same for us when we embark on a work for God. We pray, we prepare, and we dive in. And then the enemy strikes. Satan cannot stand for us to have any sort of victory as we work for God's kingdom and with His people.

This week we will see how the Jewish builders are taunted, heckled, put down, and ridiculed. This verbal attack comes from two men who stand in opposition to the wall being built. While this is a human and visible enemy, we must also know that Satan was against the work of rebuilding the wall and the reestablishment of the temple of God as well. We are looking at the deeds and actions of these two men, but please do not think for a moment that Satan was not influencing their thoughts and turning their hearts against God's people.

We will look at the men who are against Nehemiah, but we will also look at the ways these men come against those who are building the wall and compare their tactics to those of a far greater enemy—Satan. Just as those builders are working and serving God, we too should expect opposition as we live to serve God and others. We must be fully aware of the types of schemes Satan uses against us and how to respond when it happens. Satan will always try to hinder the work of God. His tactics are clever and pointed.

Satan often comes against us using the weapons of ridicule and criticism to make us cower in shame. He wants us to turn our thoughts inward. He wants us to focus on ourselves and our inadequacies rather than on God's faithfulness to see us through any difficulties or trials. If he succeeds, we will struggle to persevere in challenging times and never complete the task before us. When we are serving the Lord, we should expect opposition and keep our eyes fixed on Jesus. When we are serving the Lord and working to bring glory to His name, the enemy becomes active. Opposition from our enemy is proof that God is working in our lives, and it drives us to become laser-focused on Jesus and completely dependent on Him.

Are you prepared when the enemy strikes?

Let's see what we can learn from Nehemiah this week.

DAY 1

— READ *NEHEMIAH 2:18-20* —

1   Nehemiah has inspected the wall and determined the scope of work that needs to be done. Now he approaches those who will build the wall to get the project started and encourages the workers. Read **Nehemiah 2:18**. Under whose authority is Nehemiah working? What is the people's response to Nehemiah's leadership?

God & the King
Supportive

2   Read **Nehemiah 2:19**. What are the names of the three men who are antagonizing Nehemiah and the men building the wall? What do they do and say in opposition to Nehemiah and the workers?

Tobiah Sanballat Geshem
Samaritan, Ammonite, Areb

3   What is Nehemiah's response according to **Nehemiah 2:20**?

God is in control

4   God has given Nehemiah a job to do. He is with Nehemiah and is working through him to accomplish a magnificent work. Just like Nehemiah, it seems that when we begin a work for the Lord, Satan tries to frustrate and disrupt our plans. What encouragement do you find in the following verses?

Job 42:2

Jeremiah 29:11–13

_____

_____

_____

Philippians 1:6

_____

_____

_____

5 Which of the above verses is the most meaningful to you? Write the verse below, and insert your name.

_____

_____

_____

DAY 2
— READ NEHEMIAH 4:1-22 —

In Chapter 3, the people are all working hard on the Jerusalem wall, building the gates, and are seemingly content in their work. But ridicule and threats make their way into the people's lives through Sanballat and Tobiah, and it is affecting their lives with real consequences. While the Jews building the wall are facing a human enemy, **Ephesians 6:12** reminds us that the real battles we face are not against human foes but against the spiritual forces of darkness—in other words, Satan himself and his evil minions. We should expect opposition and know the schemes Satan uses against us. Over the next couple of days, we are going to look at some of the ways he tries to discourage us and defeat us, but do not get bogged down in the negative. Later this week, the study will focus on how we have victory over Satan through Christ Jesus. And let me assure you, we do have victory over Satan. Hallelujah!

But for today, we will see how Nehemiah's enemies use ridicule, discouragement, and fear to come against him.

1   Read **Nehemiah 4:1–3**. According to verse 1, how does Sanballat feel about the Jews rebuilding the wall, and how does he respond to them?

_____

_____

2   Ridicule is defined as "an attempt to arouse laughter or merriment at another's expense by making fun of or belittling him."[4] It is often used by people who are angry or feel the need to prove they are better than someone else. What do the following verses say about watching the tongue and controlling anger?

James 1:19–20

_____

_____

_____

James 3:7–10

_____

_____

_____

3   As Sanballat and Tobiah continue to conspire against those building the wall, discouragement begins to set in. How do you see their discouragement in **Nehemiah 4:9–10**?

_____ _complaining, task too big_ _____

_____

4   When we get discouraged, we need to focus on the hope we have been given through the power of the resurrection and the love God has shown to each of us. How are you encouraged by the verses below?

Romans 5:3–5

_____

_____

_____

Romans 15:13

_____

_____

_____

5 The enemies of Nehemiah continue their assault to the point of threatening to kill the workers. Can you imagine the fear the workers are experiencing? How does Nehemiah address their fears in **Nehemiah 4:14**?

_____

_____

_____

What does God do according to **Nehemiah 4:15**?

_____

_____

_____

6 Can you recall a time when you faced a situation where you were fearful? Read **Psalm 56:1–13**, and summarize the verses and thoughts that are meaningful and especially encouraging to you.

_____

_____

_____

DAY 3
— READ *NEHEMIAH 6:1-14* —

Satan is ultimately concerned with getting you to lower your standards and beliefs. If he can get you to compromise your standards of Christian conduct and persuade you that there is no harm in lowering those standards, then he has won a major victory. We should note that Nehemiah's enemies are very persistent. And our enemy is too.

Satan tries to do anything to intimidate us so we will give up in fear. He wants us to compromise our faith and disobey God. He hopes we will react to his schemes in fear rather than respond in faith to situations and circumstances that invade our routines. Satan knows that if he can make us afraid, he will make us ineffective.

1   Read **Nehemiah 6:1–5**. How many times do Sanballat and Tobiah attempt to get Nehemiah to compromise by sending letters and messengers?

_____

_____

_____

_____

2   In **Nehemiah 6:5–8**, Sanballat threatens to accuse Nehemiah of rebelling against the king. If this rumor reaches the king, it will be considered treason, and Nehemiah could be put to death. In **Nehemiah 6:9**, what is determined to be the purpose of their accusation?

_____

_____

_____

_____

3   Nehemiah is being falsely accused. What do you learn about this type of persecution in **Matthew 5:11–12**?

_____

_____

_____

_____

4   In **Nehemiah 6:10–14**, the enemy changes his tactic. Where does Shemaiah suggest they go to hide, and what is Nehemiah's response?

_____

_____

_____

_____

5   Why would it have been wrong for Nehemiah to enter the temple according to **2 Chronicles 23:6**? According to the account of King Uzziah in **2 Chronicles 26:16–21**, how does God respond to the king's disobedience?

_____

_____

_____

_____

_____

DAY 4
— READ AND REVIEW —
NEHEMIAH 2, 4, AND 6

Today we are going to look at how Nehemiah responds to his attackers and who he looked to for guidance, vengeance, and direction.

1 Read **Nehemiah 4:4, 4:9, 6:9, and 6:14**. What does Nehemiah do when his enemies begin to attack? In some verses, Nehemiah's action is implied. Look at who Nehemiah mentions by name to determine the implied action.

_____
_____
_____
_____
_____

2 Who is Nehemiah looking to for victory? See **Nehemiah 2:20, 4:14–15, and 4:20**.

_____
_____
_____
_____

3 Prayer is the key to victory in everything we do. We need God's wisdom, guidance, direction, and protection every day and every moment. What do the following verses say about prayer?

Psalm 4:1

_____ Hear my prayer O God _____
_____
_____

Romans 8:26–27

_____

_____

_____

Philippians 4:6–7

_____

_____

_____

4 One of my favorite verses in the entire book of Nehemiah is **Nehemiah 4:6**. Opposition is fierce, morale is low, and risk of being killed is high…"and so," what do the people do according to this verse?

_____

_____ worked with enthusiasm _____

_____

_____

5 Life can be challenging and hard at times. How do the following verses encourage you to continue when you are discouraged?

I Corinthians 15:58

_____ be strong, immovable
_____ enthusiastically for the Lord
_____ nothing for God is ever useless

James 1:12

_____

_____

_____

_____

James 5:10–11

_____

_____

_____

_____

DAY 5

— READ EPHESIANS 6:12-17 —

When it comes to experiencing spiritual warfare, discouragement, ridicule, and fear, we should not ask if we will have battles to fight but when will they come. Jesus tells us that as His children, we will experience trials, but as we consider and remember the immeasurable joy of heaven that is promised to us in Jesus, these afflictions seem minimal and only last a moment (**2 Corinthians 4:17**).

So, we prepare for battle. We know God will fight every battle for us, but we also know we bear some responsibility to stand firm in the battle. So, what should we do to prepare?

1. **Ephesians 6:12–17** lists the armor of God that we should all put on as we step into warfare. What is the protective armor listed in these verses?

   Belt of truth, body armor of God's righteousness,
   shoes of peace, shield of faith, helmet of
   salvation, sword of spirit (Word of God)

2. The list in **Ephesians 6** only includes one weapon—the Word of God (**verse 17**). What do you learn about the power of God's Word from the following verses?

   Psalm 19:7–9 ✦

   instructions are clear, perfect,
   trustworthy, insightful

   Psalm 119:105

   Your word is a lamp to guide my
   feet & a light for my path

Nehemiah - ch 3 who are your go to people?
Are you someone's go to person?
ch 4. Ridicule Has this ever happened
to you?
ch 6. Intimidation

Romans 15:4

_____
_____
_____

2 Timothy 3:16–17

_____
_____
_____

3 We also need to make sure our minds and thoughts are set on Jesus at all times. How is this expressed in the following verses?

Romans 12:2

_____
_____
_____

2 Corinthians 10:4–5

_____
_____
_____

4 In order to be prepared, we need to be in God's Word, be prayerful, guard our minds, and be quick to protect our integrity and not conform to the practices of this world. Write a prayer below telling God of your commitment to follow His ways, and ask for His protection and guidance as you live each day.

_____
_____
_____
_____
_____
_____
_____
_____
_____
_____
_____
_____

"Where do we find the power to overcome? It is found in the same place as the motive to inspire: the cross of Jesus Christ. In the cross, there is not only the mighty inspiration of the love of God but also the secret of dynamic power which can turn out sin and implant holiness in human lives. The cross is central and basic to holy living. Nobody can know what the victorious life is merely by going to Calvary to be forgiven; he must stay at Calvary until he knows something of the wounds in his own spirit, until he knows something of what it means for the Holy Spirit to crucify his lust, and his affections, and his desires.

That life which was sacrificed upon the cross, that perfect life of purity which triumphed over the grave, is now at the disposal of every believer. For by the Holy Spirit, He can enter into our hearts and live out His holiness in us. We cannot overcome, but He can! Under His authority we have the authority over the enemy. We take the words of Nehemiah out from the Old Testament into the New, and as the only basis for holiness and victory in my own life, I have to say to you, "Did not I, because of the love of Jesus." That is the only motive that can inspire a man to stay right with God, to keep his life pure and clean."[5]

—Alan Redpath

Concluding Thoughts

Ever been there? Have you stepped up in faith to try to do something for the Lord only to feel roadblocks, discouragement, and difficulties at every turn? Most likely, your task is not something as major as building a wall around a city. Sometimes just committing to attending a Bible study or volunteering for a committee or event at church can seem like an impossible task. We are all ready to get started, and then the opposition strikes. Often, we just quit.

While Satan does not know everything, he does know our weaknesses and how he has defeated us in the past. For me, it is insecurity. Just this morning I planned to attend a training for an event at my church for which I really wanted to volunteer. I signed up, but getting to the training was a major hurdle for me. Defeating thoughts made it difficult. Who will I sit with? I will be all alone. Why am I doing this? But I went, as did many friends and people I know from church. Four hundred and fifteen people attended the event, to be exact. Satan would have loved to stop me from going and serving my church. He certainly had me believing I would be all alone. What a lie! But he did not get the victory!

So how do we combat these attacks and these discouraging thoughts? How do we get past the lies our enemy is feeding us? First, we must know that as children of God we have the power to overcome any opposition that comes our way. Jesus Christ defeated the power of death and Satan on the cross, and He now lives in the hearts of every believer through the Holy Spirit. And friend, the One who is in you is far greater than the one who is in the world (**1 John 4:4**).

Second, we must be on guard at all times. Know where your walls are weak. If you love to gossip, avoid those who tempt you to talk about others or will listen to you without calling you out. If you struggle with overeating, watch what you buy in the grocery store, or do not drive by the donut shop. Ask God to be your strength, but also enlist the help of others who are strong in their faith. Nehemiah did not keep guard at the wall by himself. He enlisted the help of others. Enlist help where you need to for accountability and prayer support.

Third, you must know the truth—the Word of God. With God's truth, you will recognize the counterfeit when you see it. Every aspect of God is counterfeited by Satan. So, when Satan tries to get you to compromise your faith and beliefs in any way, recognize his attempts as a lie before you believe them. Scripture tells us that Satan will sometimes come at us like a roaring lion (**1 Peter 5:8**). But sometimes he will come at us disguised as an angel of light (**2 Corinthians 11:14**). We must be attentive and watch for his attacks.

Last and definitely most importantly, we must know Jesus Christ as our Savior. All of us must come to the place where we recognize we have done at least one thing, if not many things, that are displeasing to a holy God. These actions created a wall between us and God. We all need Jesus who paid the penalty for all our displeasing actions on the cross. Once we realize our need for a Savior, then we ask God to forgive us for everything we have done against Him and invite Jesus to come into our lives. He comes into our hearts to live—to guide us, to help us, to comfort us, and to help us fight. And He gives us the gift of living forever in heaven with Him. If you do not know Jesus as your personal Savior, please see the following page called "How to Know Jesus."

HOW TO KNOW JESUS

Sweet friend, there is no greater joy than being at peace with God and knowing that you will live in eternity with Him. Being a good person, going to church, or giving money to charities, for example, are all good things and come from a good heart. The problem is that by God's standard, good people don't go to heaven when they die. Only holy people go to heaven.

While that may sound impossible, it isn't. Every one of us has sin in our lives—things we have done that are displeasing to and disobedient to God. Whether we told a little white lie, committed a heinous crime, or did anything in between, it is all sin. And in God's eyes, the debt of sin must be paid.

And the payment for and the penalty for sin is death.

Jesus Christ was God's Son, born of a virgin. He lived a perfect and sinless life on earth for 33 years until He was crucified. Because He was a sinless, spotless sacrifice, His death paid the penalty for sin.

The question is, will you accept the death of Jesus in your place to pay the debt you owe God for your sin, or do you want to pay the debt on your own? One day, we will stand before God, and He will ask about our payment method. If you have accepted the gift of Jesus as your payment, you will enter into eternity with God. If you decided to reject Jesus and make the payment on your own by trying to be good enough to get in, God will require you to make the payment of your spiritual death for your sin—eternal separation from God in a place of torment. If you have waited until after you are face-to-face with God to call on the name of Jesus, you will be too late.

So how do you accept Jesus' death as payment for your sin now?

Simply pray the prayer below. *Prayer is simply talking with God silently or out loud.*

———————————

DEAR GOD, I ADMIT THAT I HAVE SIN IN MY LIFE AND HAVE DONE THINGS THAT ARE DISPLEASING AND DISOBEDIENT TO YOU AND YOUR WORD. PLEASE FORGIVE ME OF MY SIN. I ACCEPT THE PAYMENT THAT YOUR SON, JESUS, MADE ON THE CROSS IN MY PLACE. I ACCEPT YOUR SON AS MY SAVIOR, SAVING ME FROM BEING ETERNALLY SEPARATED FROM YOU. JESUS, PLEASE COME INTO MY HEART. AMEN.

———————————

Is it really that simple? Is it really just praying that simple prayer? Yes, it is! If you are truly sorry for your actions against God and accept the payment of Jesus to cover them, then through God's forgiveness and grace you are saved.

If you prayed this prayer, I encourage you to tell someone—a Christian friend, a pastor, a church leader, or someone else—and get connected with your local church so you can grow in your newfound salvation.

Additional Notes

_____
_____
_____
_____
_____
_____
_____
_____
_____
_____
_____
_____
_____
_____
_____
_____
_____
_____
_____
_____
_____
_____
_____
_____
_____
_____
_____

LESSON FOUR

Rest in God's Love

— NEHEMIAH 3:1-32, 7:4-73, 11:1-12:26 —

Have you ever felt like you are invisible? Has it seemed like everything was falling apart, life was too challenging, you could barely keep your head above water, and no one seemed to even notice? Maybe it is not all that bad, but just getting dinner on the table seems to be an overwhelming task, and no one is volunteering to help.

When we are in a difficult place, it can seem as if no one sees us and no one cares. I think one of our greatest emotional needs is to be seen and known. It is so discouraging when we think those we love do not understand what we are going through. It can be especially defeating during those times if we start to wrongly believe that God is oblivious to our challenges.

In **Lesson 3**, we looked at the tactics of the enemy. One tactic we did not cover was Satan's lie that we are all alone. He tries to convince us that everyone around us is doing great and that we are the only one who is struggling. Satan wants us to isolate ourselves and keep our friends or family oblivious that we are having a tough time. He hands us a shovel and hopes we will start digging a hole, a pit if you will, and then he invites us to crawl into it and be miserable.

This week, I want you to concentrate on the fact that God sees you. He created you and knows your name; He has planned every one of your days; He is familiar with your ways, your personality, and even your quirks. He knows what you are going to say before a word is even on your tongue. He knows your thoughts and your heart (**Psalm 139**). He gives you spiritual gifts, talents, and abilities, and empowers you to use them all for His kingdom and His glory. Oh, friend, He loves you!

We are also going to spend some time looking in Nehemiah at the gates that were repaired in the wall. As we look into applying the concept of building walls and gates in our own lives, it is particularly important to understand that there are many types of walls we can build. Some are healthy, and some are not. Walls are built to protect those who live inside them, and they keep the enemy out. In our lives, we also build walls of protection around our hearts and minds.

Healthy walls (maybe better-termed boundaries) are built to protect us from evil influences, guard our minds against ungodly thoughts, and keep our hearts pure. These walls must have gates so we can allow God's Word and His people into our lives. In addition, our love for others, our service for God, and our concern for the lost and hurting are all expressions that should flow from our hearts and minds through the gates of our lives and out to others. It is important to put guards over the gates of our lives to ensure that we welcome godly influences and protect our lives by keeping out sin, corruption, evil, and godlessness.

We become the gatekeepers, if you will, of these healthy walls. We determine what we let in by the choices we make. The books we read, the TV shows and movies we watch, and the places we go are just a few examples of the influences we choose to allow through the gates and into our hearts and minds. Hopefully, we make wise choices about what we allow in. The gates also allow rubbish to pass out of our lives. Impure thoughts, sinful actions, bitterness, negativity, worldliness, and the like need to be removed and taken out as trash. This is the flow of a healthy wall.

Unfortunately, life can cause us pain. People can be cruel, whether they intend to or not. Unfulfilled plans and dreams can be disappointing or even devastating. When we get hurt, we tend to build unhealthy walls and lock the gates, not allowing anyone or anything to penetrate them and not giving our hurt and pain a gate through which to escape. These are walls that should be torn down as soon as we see them in our lives. We build this type of wall to keep our emotions locked inside so we do not effectively deal with our hurt. We build this type of wall to keep others out so we feel isolated and alone. When we build a wall out of hurt, we become prisoners by walling in our emotions, which leads to bitterness, anger, and depression. This type of wall is easy to build and hard to recognize and tear down. It makes us feel safe when in reality it destroys our faith and our relationships. Oh, friend, walls built with the bricks of hurt are not protective—they are just the opposite.

As you work through this week's lesson, celebrate the wonderful, unique person God has created you to be, but also pray for His Spirit to show you unhealthy walls you may have built or gates you have locked that He wants you to unlock. He wants you to walk in freedom, and while living inside the walls may feel emotionally safe, it is not living free.

DAY 1
— READ *NEHEMIAH 3:1-32* —

1 Look at **Nehemiah 3**, and skim the verses. What is in this chapter?

_____
_____
_____
_____
_____
_____

2 I have always loved to see lists of names in Scripture. They remind me that every person is important to God and that He sees us. You are also incredibly special to God. Just as the men working on the wall were known by name, you are also known by God. He knows your name, and He loves you very much. How do the following verses indicate that you are special to God?

Isaiah 49:16

name written on His hands
_____
_____

Matthew 10:29–31

Knows our hairs & more important
than sparrows
_____

Ephesians 2:10

God's masterpiece
_____
_____

3

Read **Psalm 139:1–16**, and record verses that are especially meaningful to you in this passage.

God knows all about me,

The intricate details.

He made me.

4

Look now at another beautiful passage, **Psalm 103**, and record all that God does for you as seen in the specific verses below. These verses are such great reminders of God's love and how He is working in your life. As you work through these verses, let His truth pour over you and wash away any doubt you may have about how much you mean to Him. He loves you deeply.

Verse 3

Verse 4

Verse 5

Verse 6

Verse 8

Verse 10

_____
_____
_____

How much does God love you according to **verse 11**?

_____
_____
_____

How far does He remove your sin from you according to **verse 12**?

_____
_____
_____

Describe His compassion according to **verse 13**?

_____
_____
_____

Write a prayer to God expressing your gratefulness for all He has done for you.

_____

v.22   let all that I am praise
The Lord!

_____
_____
_____
_____
_____
_____
_____
_____
_____

DAY 2
— READ *NEHEMIAH 3:1-32* —

Today we are going to focus on the same passage of Nehemiah that we looked at yesterday but in a different aspect. Not only am I encouraged by the list of names recorded in God's Word but I also love the detail Nehemiah uses in recording, where each individual or family was working, and what work they performed. Not only was each name important but so was their specific task.

The wall built around the city was critically important to the security of the city and the protection of those who lived in it. Also important were the gates that were built into the wall. Each gate had a specific function and was opened to allow commerce and visitors into and out of the city. Gates were opened at specific times of day and closed at night. Guards were stationed at the gates for added protection.

Today we are going to focus on the names of the gates. While I do not want to over-spiritualize Scripture and look for meanings that might be a stretch, the order and names of the gates do tell a beautiful story and illustrate how God woos us and walks with us through life.

1   Read **Nehemiah 3:1**, and answer the following questions:

What is the name of the gate, and who repaired it?

_____

_____

_____

According to the chart at the end of today's questions, what was the purpose of this gate?

_____

_____

_____

What other interesting facts do you learn from the chart?

_____

_____

_____

2 Remember, the wall Nehemiah was building was to protect the city of Jerusalem, and at the center of Jewish life was the temple. So the gates in the wall reflected life in Jerusalem. This first gate was the entrance for sacrificial animals to be brought into Jerusalem and led to the temple for sacrificial purposes. In **Hebrews 9:1–15**, there is a summary of the layout of the temple and the role of the Jewish priest. Read these verses, and record anything interesting to you.

_____

_____

_____

_____

3 What do you learn about Jesus from the following verses?

Romans 3:24-26

These verses are easier to understand in the New International Version, which reads:

> "GOD PRESENTED CHRIST AS A SACRIFICE OF ATONEMENT, THROUGH THE SHEDDING OF HIS BLOOD—TO BE RECEIVED BY FAITH. HE DID THIS TO DEMONSTRATE HIS RIGHTEOUSNESS, BECAUSE IN HIS FORBEARANCE HE HAD LEFT THE SINS COMMITTED BEFOREHAND UNPUNISHED— HE DID IT TO DEMONSTRATE HIS RIGHTEOUSNESS AT THE PRESENT TIME, SO AS TO BE JUST AND THE ONE WHO JUSTIFIES THOSE WHO HAVE FAITH IN JESUS."

_____

_____

_____

John 1:29

_____

_____

_____

4   Biblical scholars who look deeply into the meaning of Scripture have seen this gate as a picture of God's provision of a Savior for us through Jesus Christ. It is where we first begin our walk with Christ by recognizing Jesus as our Savior and accepting His death on the cross as payment for our sin. Do you recall the day or the time in your life when you recognized your need for a Savior? Recount the details below.

_____

_____

_____

_____

_____

_____

5   Tomorrow we will continue to look at the gates that were built into the wall around Jerusalem. To conclude today's study, write a prayer that thanks God for His provision of the perfect Lamb, Jesus Christ, who was sacrificed for your sin.

_____

_____

_____

_____

_____

_____

Jerusalem's Walls & Gates

IN THE DAYS OF NEHEMIAH
— NEHEMIAH CHAPTER 3 —

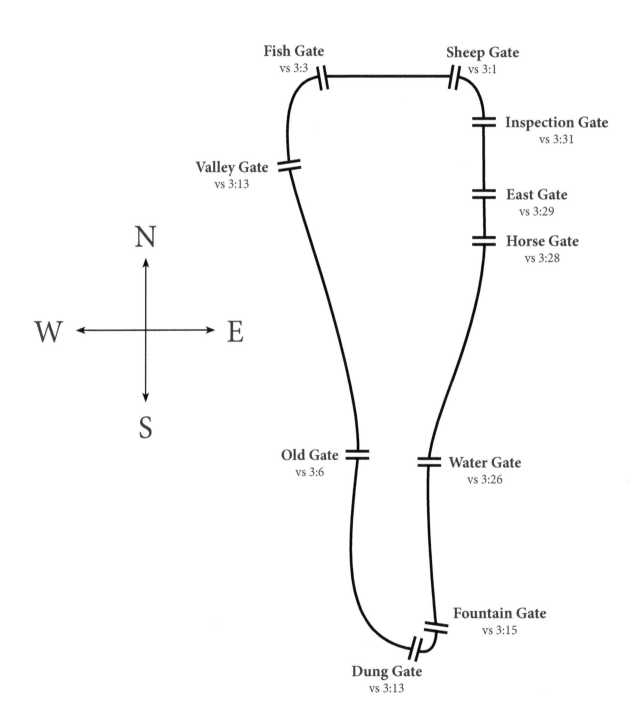

Fish Gate
vs 3:3

Sheep Gate
vs 3:1

Inspection Gate
vs 3:31

Valley Gate
vs 3:13

East Gate
vs 3:29

Horse Gate
vs 3:28

N

W — E

S

Old Gate
vs 3:6

Water Gate
vs 3:26

Fountain Gate
vs 3:15

Dung Gate
vs 3:13

Gates in Jerusalem Wall

— NEHEMIAH CHAPTER 3 —

GATE NAME	VERSE	PURPOSE	SYMBOLIZES	NT REFEENCE	INTERESTING FACTS
Sheep Gate	1, 32	bring in animals/ sacrifices	Jesus Christ	John 1:29	The only gate sanctified by priests; gate that Jesus always used to enter Jerusalem, except for Triumphal Entry; had no locks or bars, signifying the way to the Savior is never barred to anyone.
Fish Gate	3	fisherman used gate to bring in fish from the Mediterranean Sea	we are to be fishers of men	Matt 4:19	Sheep Gate is mentioned first because one must be saved before he can be a fisher of others.
Old Gate	6		old, ancient paths; paths that bring rest	2 Cor. 5:17	Also called "Jeshanah Gate;" reminder that our old nature has passed away and that we are made new in Jesus Christ.
Valley Gate	13		humility	Col 3:12	Life will have seasons where we are in the valley, but God never leaves us (**Psalm 23**).
Dung Gate	14	where filth/ garbage was carried out of the city	cleansing	1 John 1:9	Important gate for the health of the city.
Fountain Gate	15		Holy Spirit	John 7:37-39	Located near the Gihon Spring, where Jerusalem received fresh water.
Water Gate	26	used to bring water into the city	Word of God	Matt. 24:35	this gate was not repaired, suggesting that the Word of God stands forever and will not fail; Ezra erected his pulpit at this gate (**Chapter 8**).
Horse Gate	28		warfare in Christian life	2 Tim. 2:1-4	Priests also repaired this section of the gate, along with the Sheep Gate.
East Gate	29		expectancy in the return of Christ	Luke 21:28	Also called "Golden Gate;" first gate opened each morning in Jerusalem; gate Jesus used to enter Jerusalem on Palm Sunday – Triumphal Entry; gate Jesus will enter at His 2nd coming; also called "Golden Gate;" sealed shut in 1541.
Inspection Gate	31	where army was reviewed; registry	Bema judgment; rewards for faithful service given to Believers by Christ	1 Cor.3:10-15 2 Cor 5:9-10 Rom. 14:10-12	Also called "Miphkad Gate"; where visitors entering Jerusalem had to stop and register; also, where the king or commander stood to review the army before going into battle and when returning home.

DAY 3
— READ *NEHEMIAH 3:1-32* —

As believers in Jesus Christ as our Savior, we should protect our hearts and minds and remain focused on Him at all times. In **Romans 12:2** we read, "Do not be conformed to this world, but be transformed by the renewal of your mind, that by testing you may discern what is the will of God, what is good and acceptable and perfect." (ESV) God has given us so many gifts and showered us with His love, but we also have the responsibility to live a life that pleases God and to be obedient to what He asks of us.

We have seen beauty in reflecting on the picture of the Sheep Gate that represents the cross and the sacrifice of Jesus. Today we will look at the remaining gates in the wall and focus on a few of them and how they can be compared to the gateways in our own life as we keep guard of what is coming in and going out.

1. As we read **Nehemiah chapter 3**, the gates that follow the Sheep Gate are the Fish Gate and the Old Gate. In the life of the believer, these gates remind us that once we come to know Jesus as our Savior, we should be excited to tell others about Him as "fishers of men." We also should be willing to lay aside our old ways of life and walk in godliness. The Valley Gate in **Nehemiah 3:13** represents humility.

Look up the definition of humility in the dictionary, and record it here.

_____

_____

_____

What do you learn about humility from **1 Peter 5:6–7**?

humble yourself under mighty hand of God

_____

_____

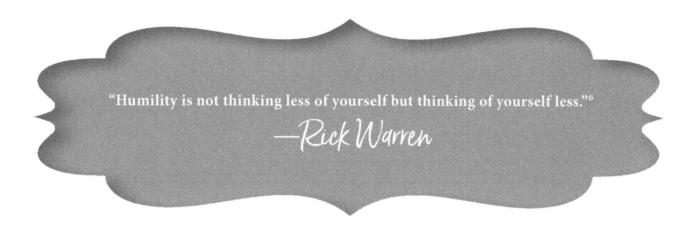

2 In **Nehemiah 3:14**, we learn of repairs to the Dung Gate. This gate was used to take the garbage out of the city. We also need to make sure the garbage of sin is taken out of our lives every day. As Christians, we know that Jesus' sacrifice on the cross paid for our sins once and for all. When we accept His gift of grace, we are forgiven of all our sins—past, present, and future—but we still sin. While daily confession is not necessary for our salvation, we need to do it to clear our conscience and restore uninhibited communion with God. What do you learn from the following verses about confessing sin and accepting forgiveness?

Psalm 32:5

Confession elimanates guilt

1 John 1:9

confession = forgiveness , cleanses us

3 Two gates have water in common. The Fountain Gate mentioned in **Nehemiah 3:15** is located in the south near the end of the Pool of Siloam. The Water Gate in **Nehemiah 3:26** is located at the Spring of Gihon where Hezekiah's tunnel begins. Water is central to sustaining life, and these gates speak of our sanctification, the work of the Holy Spirit in our lives, and our need to be refreshed daily through God's Word. What do you learn about the Holy Spirit and the Word of God from the following verses?

Psalm 18:30

God's way is perfect

Psalm 119:105

God's Word is a lamp to guide my feet & light for my path

John 14:26

Holy Spirit

Romans 8:26

Holy Spirit prays for us when we don't know how to pray.

The last gate I want to look at this week is the Inspection Gate or Muster Gate, mentioned in **Nehemiah 3:31**. This is the gate where those wishing to enter the city of Jerusalem would present their appropriate papers, showing that they were cleared to enter the city. One day you will stand at the gate of heaven. The Book of Life will be opened, and if your name is found written in it as one who has relied on Jesus for salvation, you will be welcomed into heaven. Jesus will also be coming again to earth at the end of time. What do you learn about this from the following verses?

Matthew 24:36–37

Mark 13:26

1 Thessalonians 4:13–18

_____

_____

_____

_____

5 We are to carefully guard the gates of our lives, watching what we allow in and what we quickly need to usher out of our lives. From our study today, we see that we need to open the gates wide to His Word, to the leading of the Holy Spirit, to humility, and to watchfulness for His return. We also need to rid ourselves of sin and pride. What has God shown you this week? What "gates" in your life do you need to repair?

_____

_____

_____

DAY 4
— READ *NEHEMIAH 7:4–73* —

Not only does God know your name and value you as an individual, but He has also uniquely equipped you for tasks and work during your life. Our work might be a vocation, serving in a church or parachurch ministry, or loving and serving those in our family or our community. Whatever your work, know that God has given you unique abilities and talents to accomplish it.

1 Skim through **Nehemiah 7:4–73**. Once again, we see a list of names—a census, if you will. **Verse 73** does not list names. What does it list?

_____

_____

_____

_____

_____

2

Fill in the blanks below to learn what God says about you from **Ephesians 2:10 (ESV)**.

For we are His _____, created in Christ

Jesus for _____, which God prepared

beforehand, that we should _____ in them.

How does **Psalm 139:16** explain this concept?

_____
_____
_____
_____
_____

3

According to **Philippians 1:6**, God began the work in you, but who is responsible to see it through?

_____
_____
_____

4

According to the following verses, what is the purpose of the gifts and talents God has given you?

Matthew 5:14–16

_____
_____
_____
_____

1 Peter 4:10–11

_____
_____
_____
_____

5   While God has given us gifts and talents, and promises to finish the good work He has begun in us, we are not without responsibility. What do the following verses say about our attitude in working?

1 Corinthians 15:58

_____

_____

_____

Ephesians 6:6–8

_____

_____

_____

Colossians 3:17

_____

_____

_____

Colossians 3:23–24

_____

_____

_____

6   God has given you unique talents and abilities, and He has a work for you to do for Him. He equips you and guides you along the way. Remember, He is with you. Read **Deuteronomy 31:8**. Write a prayer of thanksgiving for all God has given you, committing your work to Him.

_____

_____

_____

_____

_____

_____

_____

_____

_____

DAY 5
— READ NEHEMIAH 11:1-12:26 —

Like yesterday's lesson, we will focus on the work of the individual. The wall has been completed at this point, so the list we will look at today describes the ongoing work of the individuals who are living inside the Jerusalem wall. We also have ongoing work that we are to do for God's kingdom and His church. But God has not left us unequipped.

1   Skim **Nehemiah 11:1-12:26**. Again, we have another list of names, but in this list, we also read about specific jobs these people had. Write down some of the ways these people worked and served in Jerusalem.

_____

_____

_____

_____

_____

2   Read **1 Corinthians 12:4-11**. God gives many gifts to all believers.

According to **verse 6b**, who empowers these gifts in us?

_____

_____

_____

What is the purpose of these gifts from **verse 7**?

_____

_____

_____

_____

List the gifts you see in **verses 8–11**.

_____

_____

_____

_____

3   How does **Romans 12:4–6** speak to your uniqueness in the gifts God has bestowed on you?

_____

_____

_____

_____

4   What gifts are listed in **Romans 12:6–8**?

_____

_____

_____

_____

5   Sometimes we desire to serve God, but we have no idea how to get started. Prayerfully consider the actions listed in **Romans 12:9–13**. Is there an action that you feel God is asking you to do? Write a prayer of commitment, and ask God to enable you to complete this action.

_____

_____

_____

_____

_____

_____

_____

_____

_____

_____

_____

_____

_____

Concluding Thoughts

I love these chapters in Nehemiah. Yes, they are long lists of people we have never heard of, but they remind us of how special we are to God. Can you imagine if your name was recorded in God's Word? These lists show that individuals are important because God created them, and He also entrusts the work of His kingdom to these individuals and uniquely equips and empowers them to get the job done.

Can you see how special you are to God? **Isaiah 43** says, He has called you by name, and you are His. He has called you by name, just as He wrote the names of all the individuals in the chapters of Nehemiah we studied this week. You are His. His love for you is beyond all comprehension. He sent His only Son, Jesus, to be the sacrifice for your sins through His death on the cross.

God has a plan for your life, and He equips you uniquely with talents and spiritual gifts to be used for His glory and for the building up of the church. He gave each of us different abilities. Our job is to go to work for Him. The work may not always be easy, but He promises to be with us always. We use our gifts for the good of others and the glory of God, and He empowers and strengthens us to complete the job (**Philippians 1:6**). God created you uniquely. Celebrate that every day.

Do not make the mistake of trying to imitate others or comparing yourself to anyone else. God gives everyone unique abilities, and if Satan can get you to try to be like someone else instead of yourself, you may miss your God-given purpose. If Satan can distract us by making us look around to see how others are gifted, we will become less effective in what He has for us to do.

> "It is best to see each person's gift as a unique blend of the categories of giftedness, granted to that individual in connection with his or her traits and experiences and the needs of the church. Each believer becomes as unique spiritually as his fingerprints are physically."[7]
>
> —John MacArthur

There are many gifts, and like parts of our body, they should all work together in the church. When the Spirit of God is working in us as we use our gifts, we see the following things in the body of Christ:

- **UNITY** – we all come together as one
- **FELLOWSHIP** – we are deep, intimate, and inclusive
- **WORSHIP** – God is honored, glorified, and adored
- **EVANGELISM** – others are drawn to God
- **LOVE** — it is evident
- **OBEDIENCE** — we have a desire to obey God
- **SUBMISSION** — we follow God's lead
- **MINISTRY** — we care for the needs of others

All of us have been given at least one gift by the Holy Spirit to be used as God purposed for us. If you do not know what gift God has given to you, pray that He will reveal it to you. He wants you to know what it is so you can use it for Him. Once you believe you know what your gift is, find a place to serve where you can use it. God created you to be uniquely you. He has bestowed you with talents and spiritual gifts, and He empowers you to use those gifts and abilities for His kingdom. He sees you, He knows you, and He loves you more than you can imagine. Life may be tough sometimes, but keep your head high, and press on. He is on your side!

Additional Notes

LESSON FIVE

Adjust Your Focus

— NEHEMIAH 5:1–19 —

Nehemiah has been intently focused on building the wall. He has faced opposition to his work from those outside the wall, and now he faces a different crisis. In this chapter, he must deal with internal dissension.

In **Nehemiah 5**, we see some big issues. First, food is short due to famine. The population in Jerusalem is growing, and the people are hungry. In addition, government officials have levied very high taxes on the people. To make ends meet, people are selling their land or borrowing money. Even worse, some of the wealthy Jews are loaning money to their brothers at extremely high-interest rates, and when they aren't able to pay it back, these unscrupulous, wealthy men are taking the debtors' children as slaves. Needless to say, these people are experiencing terrible hardship. So, they cry out, and Nehemiah deals with the situation.

Often when we are in the middle of trials, persecution, difficulties, and troubles, we shift our gaze from Christ to something or someone else. And many times, our focus goes inward, and all we can see is our hurt, pain, and frustration. When we are struggling and downcast, we need to look up and look out. If God is with us, who can be against us? He holds us in the palm of His hand. Keep your eyes on Him. He's your focus. Then ask Him to show you those around you who might need your help or encouragement.

I have heard my daughter often ask, "Where is your gaze, and where is your glance?" Oh, friend, our gaze must be intently fixed first on Jesus Christ, looking to Him to guide us, strengthen us, help us, comfort us, and enable us to walk through the difficulties and joys of life. Our gaze should also be on how we can meet the needs of others around us. Jesus gave this reminder which He said was the greatest command, to "'love the Lord your God with all your heart and with all your soul and with all your mind and with all your strength.' The second is this: 'You shall love your neighbor as yourself'" (**Mark 12:30–31**).

I often find myself gazing at my troubles and only glancing at God amid the trials. When my focus shifts away from Him, my troubles become more than I can manage alone. When life is hard, remember to look up and look out.

DAY 1

— READ *NEHEMIAH 5:1-5* —

1 In **Nehemiah 5:1**, we learn of an outcry that arises from the men living in Jerusalem and their wives. Who are they crying out against?

_____

_____

_____

2 According to **Nehemiah 5:3–4**, what was happening that made them so upset?

_____

_____

_____

3 All of this resulted in the worst possible circumstance. What upsetting outcome do you learn about in **Nehemiah 5:5**?

_____

_____

_____

4 The Jewish people under Nehemiah were facing a type of hardship that most of us will never fully understand. We face our own kinds of hardships every day—financial struggles, relationship difficulties, family issues, illnesses, and employment problems, to name just a few of the things we deal with. What do you learn about hardships from the following verses?

Psalm 9:9

_____

_____

_____

Psalm 34:17

_____

_____

_____

2 Corinthians 4:16–18

_____

_____

_____

2 Corinthians 12:9–10

_____

_____

_____

James 1:2–4

_____

_____

_____

5 The people who are creating the hardship for the Israelites are the unjust Jewish leaders. Someone is considered unjust when their behavior is unfair, dishonest, or not morally sound. What does the Bible say about injustice in the following verses?

Psalm 37:1–2

_____

_____

_____

Proverbs 16:8

_____

_____

_____

6 Are you aware of people hurting around you? What are we encouraged to do in **Proverbs 31:8–9**? What are some ways you can speak out against injustice?

_____

_____

_____

DAY 2

— READ *NEHEMIAH 5:6–9* —

Some have speculated that Nehemiah was so intently focused on the task of building the wall that he did not see the injustice happening to the people of Jerusalem. Today we will look at Nehemiah's response once the situation is brought to his attention.

1   After Nehemiah hears about the hardships and injustice his people are suffering, how does he respond to the oppressors in **Nehemiah 5:6–8a?**

_____

_____

_____

How do the oppressors respond in **Nehemiah 5:8b?**

_____

_____

_____

2   Nehemiah was driven by anger that stemmed from watching innocent people being taken advantage of. Read **John 2:13–16**, which gives an account of Jesus responding in anger. Record what you learn.

_____

_____

_____

3   We can have righteous anger that is not sinful. In fact, some things should make us angry, such as people mocking God and His Word, injustice, oppression, and sin. However, we need to be sure our anger is targeted at sin and that we do not harbor that anger and allow it to turn into bitterness. What do the following verses say about anger?

Proverbs 14:29

_____

_____

_____

_____

Ephesians 4:26

_____

_____

_____

_____

Romans 12:19

_____

_____

_____

_____

4 What do the verses below tell us about God's anger?

Deuteronomy 32:35–36a

_____

_____

_____

Isaiah 1:17–20

_____

_____

_____

Psalm 30:4–5

_____

_____

_____

Psalm 145:8–9

_____

_____

_____

5 While purely speculative, I wonder if Nehemiah would have ever become aware of the injustices if the people had simply determined to suffer in silence. As I thought about this, I also wondered if people I know choose to endure hardship without making their friends or family aware of their situation. People are hurting. Sometimes life seems unfair, hardships prevail, and times are tough. The thought of a friend or family member suffering while I am unaware is sobering. In the space below, write a prayer to our Lord for eyes to see those who are wounded and suffering around you. Or if you are hurting right now, pray for courage to cry out; first to the Lord for help and second for God to provide someone to bring you a word of encouragement and help you get through this tough season.

_____
_____
_____
_____
_____
_____

DAY 3
— READ NEHEMIAH 5:10-13 —

1 According to **Nehemiah 5:10**, what does Nehemiah tell the oppressors to abandon?

_____
_____
_____

2 What are they to return? (See **Nehemiah 5:11**)

_____
_____
_____

Do they agree to do this? (See **Nehemiah 5:12**)

_____

_____

_____

3 Look up the word *usury* in a dictionary, and record the definition below.

_____

_____

_____

4 What do the following verses say about lending money and charging unfair interest?

Exodus 22:25

_____

_____

_____

Deuteronomy 23:19–20

_____

_____

_____

Leviticus 25:35–36

_____

_____

_____

5 What did Jesus say in **Matthew 5:42**?

_____

_____

_____

6 Nehemiah stands in front of the assembly and symbolically shakes his garment out before them. What does he say in **Nehemiah 5:13**?

_____

_____

_____

What is the response of the assembly?

_____

_____

_____

Do they do as they promised?

_____

_____

_____

DAY 4
— READ *NEHEMIAH 5:14-18* —

1 According to **Nehemiah 5:14–15**, what do the former governors do that Nehemiah does not?

_____

_____

_____

_____

2 What is the reason for Nehemiah choosing to do this differently? (See the last part of **Nehemiah 5:15**)

I love the way this verse reads in the New International Version (NIV), which says,

"But out of reverence for God I did not act like that."

_____

_____

_____

_____

This verse should give us the strength to face the world and choose to live differently. What are some areas where God is encouraging you to live differently? How can the phrase "I did not act like that" give you courage and strength?

_____

_____

_____

_____

_____

_____

3 Fearing God is having a proper reverence for Him. It is choosing to be obedient to Him and worshiping Him in light of knowing His attributes, character, and mighty deeds. How do the following verses in Proverbs describe "the fear of the Lord"?

Proverbs 1:7

_____

_____

_____

Proverbs 14:26–27

_____

_____

_____

Proverbs 19:23

_____

_____

_____

4 Read **Nehemiah 5:16–18,** and record the actions Nehemiah takes out of concern for the people.

_____

_____

_____

_____

_____

_____

5 Read **Philippians 2:3–8**. These verses tell us to have humility and look to the interests of other people. They also tell us that Jesus Christ is the example we should follow. While it is sometimes difficult to have the same attitude as Jesus in our interactions with others, this servant-hearted nature of Christ is a characteristic you would want God to develop in you. Using these verses, write a prayer to God and ask Him to cultivate humility and servant-heartedness in you.

_____

_____

_____

_____

_____

_____

_____

DAY 5
— READ *NEHEMIAH 5:19* —

When we go through times of trouble, we must get our focus off ourselves and on other people.

1 What does Nehemiah pray in **Nehemiah 5:19**?

_____

_____

_____

2 What do the following verses say about good works?

Matthew 5:16

_____

_____

_____

Hebrews 13:16

_____

_____

_____

Titus 3:14

_____

_____

_____

3 What do the following verses say about helping others when they are struggling?

Proverbs 3:27

_____

_____

_____

Galatians 6:2, 9–10

_____

_____

_____

1 Thessalonians 5:14

_____

_____

_____

4 Serving others sometimes requires us to sacrifice time or finances to help meet their needs. When we look to Jesus, we know He has made the ultimate sacrifice for us by going to the cross and paying the penalty for our sin with His life. Read the words He spoke in **John 15:12–13**. How do these verses encourage you to serve?

_____

_____

_____

_____

_____

5 **Luke 10:25–37** records the story of the Good Samaritan where a man shows mercy to someone in need, and Jesus tells those listening to "go, and do likewise." Pray, and ask the Lord to show you who needs your help this week. What are some practical ways you can show them mercy and help them in their struggles? Who knows? Maybe the person you are really helping is you, as you focus on helping others.

_____

_____

_____

_____

_____

_____

_____

_____

_____

_____

Concluding Thoughts

I have walked through some pretty tough days recently. I have been filled with doubt and fear, wondering if God is even aware of my pain and struggles. The tears I have shed could have filled buckets, and I have been in inner turmoil, focused on myself and my pain. My 25-year-old daughter called me out today and said, "I love you, but you are becoming obsessed with things other than Jesus." She was right. I sent her a text later that said, "I love you as my daughter, but I needed you today as my sister in Christ."

As I prayed and searched Scripture all day, God reminded me of **Romans 12:1–2** which says, "I appeal to you therefore, brothers, by the mercies of God, to present your bodies as a living sacrifice, holy and acceptable to God, which is your spiritual worship. Do not be conformed to this world, but be transformed by the renewal of your mind, that by testing you may discern what is the will of God, what is good and acceptable and perfect." I have been longing to know what His will is in my current situation, but it comes by presenting myself wholly to Him and allowing my mind to dwell on things of Him, not on the world. Am I still hurting? Yes. Am I wounded and broken? Yes. But I am expecting Him to do good things. My whole attitude changed when I shifted my focus. When times are difficult, it is easy for our thoughts to turn inward and to focus on ourselves, our pain, and our difficulties.

Because I felt I was being treated unfairly this week, I identified most with those in Nehemiah who were being oppressed. But there are more people in the story we can and should learn from. Sometimes we are the ones in challenging circumstances, but other times we are the ones creating the frustration others feel. We can also become too busy or self-focused and be completely unaware of those who are hurting around us. As you looked at these verses this week, be sure to put yourself into the shoes of all the people involved.

Can you identify with those who are being oppressed? We all have situations of difficulty and hardship. Sometimes it seems as if the world is completely against us and we do not see a solution. Financial difficulties, relationship troubles, the stress in our workplace, disagreements with those in our church—all these situations and more can pin us against the wall and make us feel like there is no way out. Remember, Satan loves to make us feel isolated and all alone in these times. Do not forget to cry out and let friends and family know of your struggles so they can help.

Are you in a leadership role? Do you see the suffering of those under your authority? How do you stand up for injustice? Are there situations where you might be acting unfairly? At times, we all need to examine our leadership styles. There are many ways that all of us are called to be leaders—as parents, as teachers, as employers, as Christians—and we should be careful to lead well and keep our eyes open to those around us who are hurting.

Are you in a position where you can truly make a difference in another person's life? What are you willing to give up or sacrifice so someone can be more comfortable? At times we must be willing to lay down our rights. Are you willing to stand up for what is right?

Life presents seasons of challenges and hardships as well as seasons of rest and sheer joy. Whatever season you may be in, let your gaze be intentionally focused on God. Ask Him to give you eyes to see those in need and a heart to meet the needs of those who are hurting. If you are hurting, cry out! Let someone know about your struggles, whether it is a friend, a family member, a pastor, a counselor, or anyone who will listen to you. People care and are willing to help once they are aware of your pain.

When you are intently focused on God and looking to the needs of others, you can persevere through any trial. Remember, you are not alone.

Additional Notes

_____
_____
_____
_____
_____
_____
_____
_____
_____
_____
_____
_____
_____
_____
_____
_____
_____
_____
_____
_____
_____
_____
_____
_____
_____
_____
_____
_____
_____

LESSON SIX

Abide in God's Word

— NEHEMIAH 8:1-9:4 —

I cannot turn to **Nehemiah 8** and not remember the first time I was called to teach this passage. As I was studying and preparing, I received a call that a precious friend's young son had been airlifted to the hospital after a drowning accident in their backyard pool. I rushed to the area hospital and sat with friends and church ministers in the waiting area. After an hour or so, this dear couple walked into the room to tell us the devastating news that their son did not survive.

My friend was a member of our Bible study class, and as we gathered the following morning, I could not teach. Our hearts were so heavy with grief and burdened for our precious friend as she dealt with the loss of her precious toddler that I had no words. For the lesson that morning, I simply sat in front of our class and read Scripture to the group. As God's Word washed over our hearts and minds, it felt as if the very breath of God was whispering across our heavy spirits, breathing comfort and peace into our grieving souls.

God's Word is powerful. No matter what situations you face in life, His Word has all the answers you need. It offers us strength, wisdom, power, encouragement, hope, and assurance, and speaks of the amazing love God has for each of us. As we turn to the eighth chapter of Nehemiah, the Israelites have completed the wall in 52 days. Now we see them come together to be refreshed and revived by God's Word. Can you imagine their exhaustion? They have been working day and night to build the wall and to protect the city from enemies. They have set the gates and posted guards, and now they need someone to minister to them. And Ezra steps forth and reads the Word of God to them, allowing God's words to bring comfort and healing to their weary souls.

We all have times of weariness. Whether it is spiritual, mental, physical, or emotional exhaustion, we need to run to God's Word so the words of God can wash over our souls and bring restoration. His Word is powerful and can transform our wearied hearts.

DAY 1
— READ NEHEMIAH 8:1-8 —

1 At which gate are the people gathered? (See **Nehemiah 8:1**) Look back at the chart in **Lesson 4** with the names of the gates and their meanings. What is the symbolism of this gate?

_____

_____

2 Read **Nehemiah 8:2–5**. To whom does Ezra read the Word of God, and how do they respond? Record any details from the passage that you find interesting.

_____

_____

_____

_____

3 The people had an emotional and physical response to hearing God's Word. Write down what you learn from **Nehemiah 8:6**.

_____

_____

_____

_____

4 In the ancient Jewish nation, members of the tribe of Levi were assigned the duties of the temple and were the religious teachers or priests. What do the Levites do to help the people according to **Nehemiah 8:7–8**?

_____

_____

_____

_____

5 The Israelites listen to the Word of God that Ezra reads to them from early in the morning to the middle of the day. They want to understand everything he reads and respond with raised hands and bowed knees. Today, many people struggle to find five minutes to read His Word. Read **Joshua 1:8**, and write a prayer below that asks God to create a hunger in you for His Word. Ask Him to give you the ability to find quality time to read it and a desire to obey what it says.

_____

_____

_____

_____

_____

_____

_____

_____

_____

DAY 2
— READ *NEHEMIAH 8:9-12* —

1 The Israelites are weeping and mourning. According to **Nehemiah 8:9**, what brings them to tears? Why do you think they have this response?

_____

_____

_____

_____

_____

2 Nehemiah responds to their mourning by telling them not to be grieved any longer and that the day is holy. What does he say their strength will be? (See **Nehemiah 8:10**)

_____

_____

_____

3 How do the following verses encourage you?

Psalm 30:11–12

_____

_____

_____

Jeremiah 31:13

_____

_____

_____

Ecclesiastes 3:1, 4

_____

_____

_____

DAY 3
— READ *NEHEMIAH 8:13-18* —

As Ezra is reading aloud, he comes to a religious festival they had long forgotten—the Feast of the Tabernacles or Booths. Immediately desiring to be obedient to God's commands, the people begin building their booths, consecrating themselves to God, and commemorating all God's goodness to the generations that went before them.

1   Read **Nehemiah 8:13–18**. What do you learn about the Feast of Booths from **Leviticus 23:33–43**?

_____

_____

_____

_____

_____

2   As the Israelites hear the Word of God, they are quick to respond to and obey what they hear. What do the following verses say about obedience?

Deuteronomy 12:28

_____

_____

_____

Ezekiel 11:19–20

_____

_____

_____

John 5:2–3

_____

_____

_____

3

What should be our response to reading and obeying God's Word according to the following verses?

Isaiah 66:2

_____

_____

_____

Jeremiah 15:16

_____

_____

_____

James 1:22–25

_____

_____

_____

4

What is God's response to our obedience according to **1 John 2:3–5**?

_____

_____

_____

_____

_____

5 Praying by using God's Word is a beautiful exercise and a way to know you are praying according to His will. Using the verses in **Psalm 119:97–105**, write a prayer to the Lord.

Psalm 119:97 says, "Oh how I love your law! It is my meditation all the day."

Here's a sample prayer you could write from that verse:

Oh Father, may my love for Your Word increase. Help me find time to read my Bible, and please bring scripture to my mind throughout this day so I will meditate on what it says continually.

Continue with the remaining verses using your words and your desires as you come to God in prayer.

_____

_____

_____

_____

_____

_____

_____

_____

_____

_____

_____

_____

_____

_____

_____

_____

_____

_____

DAY 4
— VARIED PASSAGES —

Today we are going to concentrate on the ways Scripture affects our lives.

1 Read **2 Timothy 3:16-17** in the English Standard Version (ESV), and fill in the blanks below:

> _____ Scripture is _____ out by _____
>
> and profitable for _____,
>
> for _____, for _____,
>
> and for _____ in righteousness,
>
> that the [wo]man of God may be _____,
>
> equipped for _____ good work.

2 Using a dictionary, define the following words:

Teaching

_____

_____

_____

Reproof

_____

_____

_____

Correction

_____

_____

_____

Training

_____

_____

_____

3

Psalm 19:7–11 describes God's Word in beautiful ways. Use your Bible to fill in the blanks using the ESV. We are going to dissect this passage into categories, so you will use the verses several times.

God's Word is described as:

Verse 7:

The _____ of the Lord is _____.

The _____ of the Lord is _____.

Verse 8:

The _____ of the Lord are _____.

The _____ of the Lord is _____.

Verse 9b:

The _____ of the Lord are _____,

and _____ altogether.

Verse 10:

More to be _____ are they than

_____ also than _____ .

How God's Word impacts me:

Verse 7:

_____ the soul making _____ the simple

Verse 8:

_____ the heart _____ the eyes

Verse 11:

by them is your servant _____ ;

in _____ them there is great

_____ .

4 Looking back over today's questions, what have you learned about God's Word? What was particularly meaningful to you in your study?

_____

_____

_____

_____

DAY 5

─ READ NEHEMIAH 9:1-4 ─

This section begins with the Israelites dressing in sackcloth and putting ashes on their heads as a sign of mourning for their sin. As they come before Ezra, they read God's Word for a quarter of the day and then confess and worship for another quarter of the day. The Israelites are truly broken. They are confronted with their sin and the sin of the generations before them, and they confess that sin before God.

1 The Jewish people are all assembled. According to **Nehemiah 9:1**, they are fasting and wearing sackcloth and ashes, which was customary during times of mourning and to show submission. What does this lead you to believe about their response to hearing God's Word?

_____

_____

_____

_____

2 What actions are described in **Nehemiah 9:2-4**?

_____

_____

_____

3 The Psalms is one of my favorite books of the Bible, especially when I am struggling with issues of the heart. It is filled with emotion, from the highest of highs to the lowest of lows. Read **Psalm 139:23-24**, which is an honest prayer. What is David asking of God in these verses?

_____

_____

_____

_____

4 Are you willing to pray a prayer as David did? Are you willing to ask Him to search your life for anything offensive to Him and show you what is not pleasing to Him? It can be scary (maybe terrifying) to ask, but it is a necessary prayer if we want to grow in our faith and have a deeper relationship with God. Write a prayer that asks God to search your heart and show you how you need to repent and ask for His cleansing and forgiveness.

_____

_____

_____

5 **Psalm 51** is a beautiful prayer and praise written by King David where he confesses his sin and experiences God's forgiveness. Read **Psalm 51:1–12**, and record the verses that speak of God's ability to forgive and cleanse us from our iniquity.

_____

_____

_____

_____

6 The Bible contains God's words to His children, but more specifically it is His love letter to us. He communicates His love, His concern, His desires, His will, and His expectations for us. As we close this week's study, write a prayer that expresses your gratitude to God for His Word and its power in your life.

_____

_____

_____

_____

_____

_____

_____

_____

_____

_____

_____

_____

Concluding Thoughts

Our Bible is such an amazing gift. It contains the very words of God spoken to His servants who wrote down and recorded all God placed in their minds and hearts. Scripture describes the character, nature, and personality of God. If we want to know Him, we read His Word.

Not only does Scripture describe who God is but it also shows us what God does and how He wants us to live. It gives us laws and regulations for government and guidelines for daily living. It gives us the keys to righteous and victorious living.

Most importantly, Scripture gives us the portrait of our Messiah in prophecy throughout the Old Testament and the beautiful reality of the Messiah in the New Testament. We learn how much God loves us and sent His Son to die for us. Most importantly, God's Word tells us how we can know our Savior, receive forgiveness of our sins, and secure the promise of eternal life (**1 John 5:13**).

According to the Wycliffe Dictionary of Theology, 'confession' is defined as an "…acknowledgment of the sovereignty of God. It is the admission of guilt when confronted with the revealed character and will of God…"[8] That is exactly what took place in the passage we studied this week. Ezra read the Word of God, and the Israelites saw God's character revealed. When they were confronted with the holiness of God, they recognized their own sinfulness and confessed and repented of their sins.

Likewise, when we are confronted with sin in our lives, we also need to confess it. By confessing, God is not going to be surprised. He has seen all our deeds, and He knows the attitudes of our hearts. **Psalm 139:4** says that even before a word is on our tongues, God knows what we are going to say. He is intimately acquainted with you, and He longs for fellowship with you.

Confession is not for God. He is well aware of our shortcomings. Confession is for you and for me to clear our consciences, remove our guilt, and give us freedom in our relationship with Him. When we stand before Him with the burden of our sin removed, we can clearly see Him in His glory and beauty, and our praise of Him cannot help but flow from our hearts. This is what we will study in the next lesson.

Additional Notes

_____
_____
_____
_____
_____
_____
_____
_____
_____
_____
_____
_____
_____
_____
_____
_____
_____
_____
_____
_____
_____
_____
_____
_____
_____
_____
_____
_____
_____
_____
_____
_____
_____
_____

LESSON SEVEN

Praise God

— NEHEMIAH 9:4-37 —

It is so important that we learn to consistently cling to the Word of God in good times and bad times. His Word should be a continual light for our path as we walk through life. His Word should show us our sins and encourage us to obey God. We have been following the lives of those who are building the wall and living in Jerusalem. We have seen how they are moved to tears upon hearing the Word of God, and we have witnessed them confessing their sins and forgetfulness of God's ways. And now they are praying from a clean heart and a clear conscience.

Nehemiah 9 records the longest prayer in the entire Bible. It includes a beautiful summary of Old Testament history but also focuses on the character of God. Because the Israelites stood cleansed before God and were in a right relationship with Him, they were able to see God for who He was and who He still is.

This week, we will be focusing on the characteristics of God that are in **Nehemiah 9**. It is definitely not an exhaustive list of all the wonderful attributes of God, but it is a list to get us started. When times are difficult, it is so easy to turn our focus from God to ourselves.

No matter how we feel, no matter how difficult life can seem at times, and no matter how we act, we cannot change who God is. He is worthy of our praise.

Before beginning the study questions this week, read **Nehemiah 9:4–37**. Underline the characteristics of God you see in this passage.

DAY 1
— READ *NEHEMIAH 9:5-6* —

1

According to **Nehemiah 9:5**, how do the Levites begin their prayer?

_____

_____

_____

_____

2 From **Nehemiah 9:6**, what are the ways that they acknowledge God?

_____

_____

_____

_____

3 Prayer begins with recognizing God for who He is. In other words, what is true about His character? While many verses speak of the character of God, what do you learn from just the few listed below?

Psalm 86:15

_____

_____

_____

Psalm 89:14

_____

_____

_____

Isaiah 40:28

_____

_____

_____

Revelation 4:8

_____

_____

_____

4 Our world is filled with many religions, humanist thinking, and self-exaltation. How do the following verses establish God's preeminence over all things and mankind's limited thinking?

1 Kings 8:22–23

_____

_____

_____

2 Kings 19:15

_____

_____

_____

Ephesians 4:6

_____

_____

_____

5   Consider the majesty, beauty, power, strength, and supremacy of God. I am awed that the God of the universe loves us. Reflect on the priorities of your life. Is God your number-one priority? Is He even in the top five? God is above all things and should be above all things in your life. Acknowledging His supremacy in your life, what commitments would you like to make before Him right now? Are you willing to make Him your priority every day?

_____

_____

_____

DAY 2
— READ NEHEMIAH 9:8 —

I love people who are true to their word. We know the people we can trust and those we cannot, and I love that God is trustworthy. When He says in **Hebrews 13:5** that "I will never leave you," we can trust Him. When He promises to give us strength, He will. When He says He will give eternal life to those who put their faith in Jesus, He will. We can trust Him because it is impossible for God to lie (**Hebrews 6:18**).

1   Record the phrases from **Nehemiah 9:8** that speak of the trustworthiness of God.

_____

_____

2 How do the following verses encourage you regarding God's faithfulness?

Deuteronomy 7:9

_____

_____

_____

2 Samuel 22:31

_____

_____

_____

Titus 1:2 (concentrate on the middle of the verse)

_____

_____

_____

3 When our circumstances are difficult and we find ourselves in times of trouble or suffering, it can be challenging to trust God. Sometimes we bring difficulties on ourselves by stepping outside of God's will or by being disobedient to His Word, but trials can also come when we are tightly tucked inside His will. Suffering can come because God is pruning us in order to develop our character. Or suffering can come because Satan is sending fiery darts aimed at our hearts. What are we instructed to do according to **1 Peter 4:19**?

_____

_____

_____

4 Below are just a few promises of God. How do they encourage you, especially when you are weary?

Exodus 14:14

_____

_____

_____

Isaiah 41:10

_____

_____

_____

Matthew 11:28–29

_____

_____

_____

5 What have you learned about the trustworthiness of God, and how has studying His faithfulness encouraged you today?

_____

_____

_____

_____

DAY 3
— READ *NEHEMIAH 9:9* —

In an attempt to explain her tears on our wedding day, my husband's precious grandmother looked at me and said, "My heart is so filled with joy that it is overflowing down my cheeks." I love that description. There was no reason for her to try to justify her tears. I embrace tears because they often flow down my cheeks. Sometimes my tears are an expression of joy and delight; other times, they are the overflow of a heart filled with sorrow and pain. Whether you cry easily or are a person who keeps your emotions to yourself, God knows your heart, sees every tear, and hears even the silent cries deep within you.

1 **Nehemiah 9:9** refers to the days of Moses when the Jewish nation was in captivity in Egypt. What does this verse say that God saw and heard?

_____

_____

_____

_____

2 Often when we are in pain, we want to be seen and be heard. From the verses below, record what God sees or hears.

Psalm 18:6

_____

_____

_____

Psalm 31:7

_____

_____

_____

Psalm 77:1

_____

_____

_____

3 What beautiful thoughts did David write in **Psalm 56:8**?

_____

_____

_____

_____

_____

4 On difficult days, how can the following verses encourage you?

1 Peter 1:3–7

_____

_____

_____

2 Corinthians 4:16–18

_____

_____

_____

5 I absolutely love the idea that God stores my tears in a bottle and records them. Sometimes our tears are for very real and painful situations, and sometimes they seem rather silly and trivial, but it does not matter to God. All our tears matter enough for Him to catch them and save them. Do you realize how near He must be to catch those tears? That is the ultimate picture of a caring father, one who cares enough to be that close and cares enough to save each tear that trickles down my face. Using the space below, reflect on what the closeness of God means to you and how much you mean to Him that He would store your tears.

_____

_____

_____

_____

DAY 4
— READ *NEHEMIAH 9:12-20* —

1 Recounting how God was with the Jewish nation as they wandered in the wilderness after leaving Egypt, what characteristic of God do you see in **Nehemiah 9:12**?

_____

_____

_____

2 **Nehemiah 9:15** speaks of the provision of God. What does it say He did for the Jews?

_____

_____

_____

3 What do you learn of God's character from **Nehemiah 9:20a**?

_____

_____

_____

4 Read **Proverbs 3:6**. Can you recall a time when you trusted God to lead you, provide for you, and instruct you? What were the circumstances, and how did trusting Him make your path straight?

_____

_____

_____

5 I cannot think of a more beautiful picture of a leader, provider, and instructor than a shepherd. Reflect on this picture of God's love for you as your Shepherd in **Psalm 23**. Insert your name in the blanks. Really think about each sentence and the truth in it.

The Lord is _____'s shepherd; (s)he shall not want.

He makes _____ lie down in green pastures.

He leads _____ beside still waters. He restores

_____'s soul. He leads _____

in paths of righteousness for his name's sake.

Even though _____ walks through the valley of the

shadow of death, _____ will fear no evil, for You

are with _____. Your rod and your staff, they

comfort _____

You prepare a table before _____ in the presence

of her/his enemies. You anoint _____'s head with

oil; her/his cup overflows.

Surely goodness and mercy shall follow _____ all

the days of her/his life, and _____ shall dwell in

the house of the Lord forever.

DAY 5

— READ *NEHEMIAH 9:17* —

Today we will look at a few more attributes of God in **Nehemiah 9**. I delight in the patience of God. He is slow to anger, and He is patient with me even when I am disobedient and stubborn, and when I think I know better and try to do things my own way. **Nehemiah 9:17–30** repeatedly records when the Israelites failed God. Over and over, we see that God gave to them, warned them, and provided for them; and over and over they rejected Him. But God was patient with them—and He is patient with us.

God's love is amazing. In Hebrew, the word *chesedh* is translated as love or loving-kindness. It speaks of an act of kindness, love, or mercy shown to someone such as a close friend or family member. And the choice of extending this love is determined by the one who is showing the love. God saw the hearts of the Israelites as they disobeyed, rebelled, and walked out of fellowship with God, and He chose to treat them as if a strong, loving relationship still existed. They wanted nothing to do with God, and He extended love to them anyway. It was His choice. The same is true today. He is constantly extending His love to us even when we have done nothing to deserve it. And His patience and love are worthy to be praised!

1. Record the attributes of God that you see in **Nehemiah 9:17**.

_____

_____

_____

2. The first characteristic listed is "forgiving." What does **Psalm 86:5–6** say about God's forgiveness?

_____

_____

_____

_____

3   I have heard grace described as receiving a gift we do not deserve, while mercy is not receiving the punishment we do deserve. What do the following verses say about God's mercy and grace?

Isaiah 30:18

_____
_____
_____

Ephesians 2:4–5

_____
_____
_____

4   Read **2 Peter 3:9**, and then write it below, inserting your name.

_____
_____
_____
_____
_____

5   **First Corinthians 13** is a familiar passage on love, and **1 John 4:8** tells us that God is love. Write **1 Corinthians 13:4–6** below, inserting God's name in place of the word "love" or "it".

_____
_____
_____
_____
_____
_____
_____
_____
_____
_____
_____
_____

Concluding Thoughts

The past two lessons really go together. We must look intently into God's Word to get a picture of who He is and who we are in comparison. We look at His holiness, and we are painfully aware of our sinfulness. We repent of our sin, and then with a clean heart and a clear conscious, we can see His character and His works even more clearly. Once we are focused on God and see Him for who He is, our praises cannot help but flow outward and upward.

Do you know God? Oh, maybe you have a personal relationship with Him and know you will go to heaven to be with Him one day, but do not really see Him as He is. To do that, we must be in a position to see Him in truth and up close. We cannot get the full picture if we are looking from behind a wall of sin.

We are fairly good at praying a simple prayer, asking God to forgive our sins, and spending a few minutes telling Him we are sorry but not recounting any specific sin. How often are we truly devastated over our disobedience? How often do we look deeply into our lives and hearts to see what God sees? I am talking about a sincere heart examination like David prayed in **Psalm 139**. Have you asked the Lord to search you and see if there is any offensive way in you? (See **Lesson 6** if you want to revisit this concept in more depth.)

Once we have examined our hearts and received the forgiveness God has to offer, we can see Him clearly. We can see His greatness, feel His leadership, know His forgiveness, hear His instruction, and experience His love in a way like never before.

God loves you totally and unconditionally. When my girls were young, I often reminded them that my love for them was not based on what they did and that they could not do anything that could make me love them any more or any less. I love my children simply because of who they are and because they are mine.

You can rest assured that God says the same thing to you; His love is not based on what you have done. You cannot make Him love you any more or any less. He loves you simply because you are His. And in that love, He sees you and hears your cries to Him. He is a good Father.

God's love for you is immense, but remember, good fathers also discipline their children when they are disobedient. When we sin, God's forgiveness will cover that sin so our position with God— our holiness and righteousness—is unchanged. But we may still experience God's discipline as a consequence of our disobedience. Yes, God loves you more than you can imagine, but in His love, He works in your life to root out sin, bad attitudes, impurities, and imperfections. As He works in you to make you look more like Jesus, it might hurt, but He is making you better because He loves you.

> "God sees us as we are, loves us as we are, and accepts us as we are. But by His grace, He does not leave us as we are."[9]
>
> —Timothy Keller

When times are good or when times are challenging, worshiping and praising God should be our priority. I hope you have focused on Him this week and seen many ways that He is worthy of our praise. Just in **Nehemiah 9**, I found the following characteristics of our God:

exalted above all (v. 6)	instructor (v. 20)
creator (v. 6)	giving (v. 20)
covenant maker (v. 8)	sustainer (v. 21)
promise keeper (v. 8)	subdues our enemies (v. 24)
righteous (v. 8)	disciplines us (v. 27)
sees and hears our cries (v. 9)	rescuer (v. 27)
leader (v. 12)	patient (v. 30)
lawgiver (v. 13)	merciful (v. 31)
provider (v. 15)	great (v. 32)
forgiving (v. 17)	mighty (v. 32)
gracious (v. 17)	awesome (v. 32)
compassionate (v. 17)	just (v. 33)
slow to anger (v. 17)	faithful (v. 33)
abounding in love (v. 17)	good (v. 35)

How awesome is it that this list is not even close to being complete?

God is amazing and definitely worthy of our praise!

Additional Notes

_____
_____
_____
_____
_____
_____
_____
_____
_____
_____
_____
_____
_____
_____
_____
_____
_____
_____
_____
_____
_____
_____
_____
_____
_____
_____
_____

LESSON EIGHT

Stand Strong

— NEHEMIAH 9:38–10:38; 13:1–30 —

In the story of the Israelites' return to Jerusalem after their years of captivity in Babylon, we have seen many amazing spiritual highs. We have seen them gather at the Water Gate and listen to Ezra the priest read from God's Word, and we have seen them obey what they heard. We have seen their deep brokenness over sin, and we have seen them confess their sins and acknowledge God's character in a new and personal way. In our study this week, we will see the action they take because of the revival that has taken place in their hearts and lives. They will stand before the Lord and sign their names in a pledge to be obedient to His law. They will make a promise before God believing they will always be faithful to that commitment.

Each of the four years I was in high school, I attended a one-week summer church camp that was the highlight of the year. We heard powerful messages from amazing speakers, and we sang praises to Jesus at the top of our lungs. We were filled with a renewed fire to live for Jesus in the coming year. Students at that camp poured down the aisles of the outdoor worship center to recommit their lives to Jesus and promise to live for Him with abandon and passion. And then camp was over and school started, and those passionate commitments often fell by the wayside.

> "It is one thing to say a prayer of passionate confession…and quite something else to live an obedient life after we say 'Amen.'"[10]
>
> —*Warren Wiersbe*

As we look at the Israelites in these passages, we will see that same passion and zeal in their desire to follow God. In contrast, we will see them fall into the very sin they promised not to commit. We will see evidence that they intended to be obedient after the "amen," and yet over time their desires are replaced, temptation comes, and the people find themselves in disobedience.

DAY 1

— READ *NEHEMIAH 9:38-10:27* —

In **Lesson 7**, we saw how beautifully the Israelites praised God for His greatness and all He had done. Acknowledging God and seeing Him as The Highly Exalted One made the Israelites desire to pledge their commitment to their awesome God. Eighty-four men put their seal on the covenant they made before God, but there were most likely many more who committed to obeying, including women and children. The act of putting a seal on a document or pledge was a very serious matter. It meant taking a solemn oath before the Lord.

Our obedience should be a joyful response to the things we see that God has done for us and motivated by our love for Him rather than fear. When we are serious about our relationship with God, we will have the desire to be submissive to His Word.

1. According to **Nehemiah 9:38**, what are the details of the commitment the people made, and how was it recorded?

_____

_____

_____

_____

_____

2. **Nehemiah 10:1–27** is the list of all the men who made this commitment and signed the document. How serious is it to make a vow before the Lord according to **Numbers 30:2**?

_____

_____

_____

_____

_____

3. What commandments are in the New Testament regarding oaths?

Matthew 5:33–37

_____

_____

_____

James 5:12

_____

_____

_____

4. Read **Numbers 3:19**. What do you learn about God's ability to keep His promises?

_____

_____

_____

_____

_____

5. What promise of God in Scripture is your favorite? How have you seen God use this promise in your life? (If you are unsure where to find God's promises in Scripture, use your Internet search engine to query "Bible verses containing God's promises." Then look up those references in your Bible.)

_____

_____

_____

_____

_____

_____

Write your promise verse below, and memorize it this week.

_____

_____

_____

_____

_____

_____

DAY 2

1   Read **Nehemiah 10:28–29 and 31**. **Verse 28** tells us that the people have separated themselves from other nations and unto the Law (God's Word). What do the people promise to do according to **verses 29 and 31**?

_____

_____

_____

2   What do you learn about being obedient to God's Word from the following verses?

Deuteronomy 12:28

_____

_____

_____

Ezekiel 20:19–20

_____

_____

_____

Ezekiel 36:26–27 *(note also who helps us obey)*

_____

_____

_____

3   The Sabbath is a day of rest when we worship God and focus on Him throughout the day. It is a day that should look different than the other days of the week. For the Jews, this is observed from sundown on Friday to sundown on Saturday. For Christians, we observe a day of rest and worship on Sunday in remembrance of the Lord's resurrection day. While the day of the week may be different, the principle is the same. What do the following verses say about keeping the Sabbath?

Exodus 20:8–11

_____

_____

_____

Exodus 31:13

_____

_____

_____

Leviticus 19:30

_____

_____

_____

4 As we jump ahead and look at **Nehemiah 13**, it is important to note that quite a bit of time has passed—about 12 years. Have the Israelites been faithful to fulfill their promise and oath? Read **Nehemiah 13:15–22**, and record what has happened.

_____

_____

_____

_____

_____

"In our family, my wife and I try to follow the simple principle of not doing on Sundays whatever could be done on any other day of the week, things like mowing the lawn, washing the car, shopping, and so on. The home didn't become a prison, but neither did it turn into a circus."[11]

—_Warren Wiersbe_

5 How I wish I could say I have been faithful to every promise I have ever made to God. It seems so easy to cry out to Him and pledge our renewed desire to be faithful to Him and His Word, especially when we are in trouble and want His help to solve our problems. We promise we will pray more, read our Bibles more, and honor Him more in our lives. And without any thought of breaking our promise, we find ourselves skipping our morning prayer time and forgetting to read our Bibles. We miss church on Sundays because other commitments or obligations become our priority, or we decide to sleep in because we are just too tired. For the Israelites, keeping the Sabbath showed they were subject to God's authority and desired to obey God's Law. Considering this concept of authority, to what or to whom do you give authority in your life regarding your Sabbath (the day dedicated to worshiping God)? What can you do to make your Sundays reflective of your commitment to God rather than look like any other day of the week?

_____

_____

_____

_____

_____

DAY 3
— READ *NEHEMIAH 10:30-31, 13:23-30* —

The Israelites committed to remaining separated and not intermarrying with anyone outside the Jewish nation. God asked them to draw a line in the sand and not cross it. Mosaic Law prohibited the Israelites from living like their Gentile neighbors, but it did not prevent them from being kind to them or doing business with them.

"Separation is simply total devotion to God, no matter what the cost."[12]

—Warren Wiersbe

1 Looking again at the oath the Israelites signed, what do they commit to doing according to **Nehemiah 10:30**?

_____

_____

_____

_____

2 Using the following verses, why do you think God wanted to keep His children separated from foreigners or Gentiles?

Leviticus 20:26

_____

_____

_____

_____

Deuteronomy 7:3–4

_____

_____

_____

_____

1 Kings 11:1–8

_____

_____

_____

_____

3 According to **Nehemiah 13:23–27**, do the Israelites keep their commitment? Describe what they had done.

_____

_____

_____

How does Nehemiah correct the situation in **Nehemiah 13:30**?

_____

_____

_____

4   As Christians, we are made pure and holy through the forgiveness of our sin by the death of Jesus Christ on the cross as He paid the penalty we deserved because we disobeyed God. Because of God's grace and Jesus' sacrifice on our behalf, our command in the New Testament is to lead lives that are worthy of being in God's family, lives that are worthy of being called a son or daughter of the King of kings, lives that reflect our gratefulness to Him and our desire to honor Him in everything we do. How is that reflected in the following verses?

Ephesians 4:1–3

_____

_____

_____

Colossians 1:9–14

_____

_____

_____

5   I was very disheartened when I read in **Nehemiah 13:24** that because of the sin of the fathers, their children did not know the Hebrew language. This language barrier prevented the children from hearing the Word of God or the messages of the priests. The fathers' sins had a profound effect on their children. I was struck by the idea that I could experience the consequences of my sin, and others around me could also suffer because of my choices. We must be committed to live lives worthy of our calling in Jesus Christ as beloved children of God. Ideally, we should be willing to be separated from the world, no matter the cost. We should want to protect our lives from corruption and worldliness and keep our lives pure. Read **1 John 2:15–17**, and then answer the following questions:

Is there anything in your life that God would ask you to give up?

_____

_____

_____

Are there any deep friendships you are cultivating that lead you into worldliness rather than godliness?

_____

_____

_____

Are there any commitments you need to give up to have more time for God?

_____

_____

_____

Are you willing to separate yourself from the world, no matter the cost?

_____

_____

_____

DAY 4
— READ NEHEMIAH 10:32-38, 13:10-14 —

Today we will look at the ways the Israelites promise to take care of the house of God. The people are also promising to meet the ministry needs of the temple. Likewise, we should want to care for our church, pray for its leaders, and give financially to its ministries and endeavors.

1

Read **Nehemiah 10:32–38**. What do the people promise to do?

_____

_____

_____

2

The temple tax was collected from the people to provide for the upkeep of the temple and the living expenses of the priests who lived and worked in the temple. What do you learn about this tax from the following verses?

Exodus 30:13–16

_____

_____

_____

Matthew 17:24–27

_____

_____

_____

3 The offering of the firstfruits reminded the Israelites to bring God their first and their best. What do you learn about the offering of the firstfruits from these verses?

Leviticus 23:9–14

_____

_____

_____

_____

_____

Deuteronomy 26:1–10

_____

_____

_____

_____

_____

4 Read **Nehemiah 13:10–14**. Years later, were the people faithful to their pledge?

_____

_____

_____

_____

_____

What were the people doing?

_____

_____

_____

_____

_____

What did Nehemiah do about it?

_____

_____

_____

_____

5   When we look at the temple tax and the offering of the firstfruits, we should be reminded that God has redeemed us with a price, His own Son, to set us free. We have been saved from death, so we should honor God with our first and our best. When we come to His house, we give Him our best in our service, no matter our task. Write a prayer of thankfulness for all God has done to redeem you, including a commitment to honor Him to the best of your ability in all you do.

_____

_____

_____

_____

_____

_____

_____

_____

_____

_____

_____

_____

"We make a living by what we get, but we make a life by what we give."[13]

—*Winston Churchill*

DAY 5
— READ NEHEMIAH 13:4-9 —

In **Nehemiah 13** we see that the Israelites neglected the house of God. They had quit tithing and giving offerings; they had not taken care of their priests and musicians. With time, the neglect had left God's house empty. Because of the emptiness, the enemy was able to move in.

1 Read **Nehemiah 13:4–9**. According to **verses 4 and 5**, what happens during Nehemiah's absence?

_____

_____

_____

_____

Looking at **verses 8 and 9**. What does Nehemiah do?

_____

_____

_____

_____

2 Do you remember Tobiah from our previous studies? (See **Nehemiah 2:10, 4:7–8**) He is an enemy of those who are building the wall and the people living in the city. Now look at where he is! Because of neglect, the house of God is empty, and the enemy has moved in. How does **Ephesians 3:16–21** encourage you to keep your life filled with the things of God?

_____

_____

_____

_____

3 Read **Colossians 3:1–17**. Write down the phrases that encourage you to lead a godly life. (You can also write these verses as a prayer and ask for His strength to live out your faith or commitment to Him.)

_____

_____

_____

_____

4 Just as Nehemiah removed Tobiah's furniture from the temple, we also need to push things out of our lives that hinder our walk with Christ. According to **Ephesians 4:22–31**, what are some of the actions and attitudes we need to rid ourselves of?

_____

_____

_____

5 Living a godly life can be difficult. It requires us to remain focused and dependent on God at all times. How do the following verses remind you of God's power and ability to strengthen you?

Psalm 73:26

_____

_____

_____

John 14:26

_____

_____

_____

Philippians 1:6

_____

_____

_____

Philippians 4:19–20

_____

_____

_____

6 It is pretty easy to begin to neglect the things of God. It starts with such a small compromise, and then suddenly, the enemy has moved in! We must be willing to stand, not in our own strength, but in His strength. Then we will see victory and be able to persevere when difficulties come our way. Write a prayer below, asking God to strengthen your resolve to live every day, every moment with complete reliance upon His strength, wisdom and power, rather than trying to depend on your own abilities.

_____

_____

_____

_____

_____

_____

_____

Concluding Thoughts

The Israelites started out well in **Nehemiah 10**. We see them wholeheartedly committing themselves to God and His service, but just a few years after their pledge, they are living their lives completely forgetting the God who gave them that life.

Twelve years have passed since the wall was built. During that time, Nehemiah returned to King Artaxerxes, and Jerusalem slipped from being a city devoted to serving and praising God to a city that looked like any other town. The people have forgotten the promises they made when they finished the wall. Their godly intentions have given way to compromises.

At the beginning of this lesson, I mentioned my high school camp experience every summer and the year that followed. The Israelites also experienced a spiritual high. The wall was built, the priests read and taught God's Word, the choirs sang, and revival broke out. But as the emotions of revival faded, the Israelites became comfortable. They enjoyed the safety of living inside the wall, and they enjoyed their prosperity and success. But they forgot the One who made it all happen.

Before we get all judgmental toward the Israelites, we should remember that we do the same thing. We go to camps and conferences or hear a sermon that truly pierces our hearts. In the emotions of that moment, we think, "Wow, life is really going to be different now!"

Then we leave the place of our spiritual revival and return to our normal activities. We are strong in our resolve to fulfill our commitment to God, but eventually, our old habits, old ideas, and old friends call us back to our old comfortable way of life. And before we know it, we have moved "Tobiah" into the place reserved for God.

What "Tobiah" has crept into your life and needs to go? It may be beautiful. It may be functional. It may be something that is in all your friends' lives. But is it taking up space that God needs, and is it time to get it out of your life? These things often seem to be good and useful, but they prevent the Holy Spirit from having the freedom to fully work in our life.

While I'm sure there are many reasons for the Israelites' failures, I did note that nowhere in this passage does it mention that they called on God to give them the strength to live out such a lofty pledge. How often do we do the same thing? We commit to getting up 30 minutes early every day to have a quiet time alone with God. We decide to begin a Bible study and say we are going to be a shining Christian example in our non-Christian world. We want to lead others to faith in Jesus Christ. But how often does this newfound commitment last about five minutes before we fail miserably?

We must rely on God to give us the strength to do these things. It must be in His strength and not in ours because we will fail miserably at anything we attempt to do in our own flesh. Each commitment, each task, each day, each moment must be lived as Paul said, "I can do all things through Him [Christ] who strengthens me" (**Philippians 4:13**).

If we are going to persevere through the tough times in our lives, we must rely on His strength to remain steadfast and stand strong.

Additional Notes

_____
_____
_____
_____
_____
_____
_____
_____
_____

LESSON NINE

Surrender in Worship

— NEHEMIAH 12:27–47 —

In **Lesson 7**, we looked at the attributes of God and how, when times are hard and even when they are not, we should lift our voices in prayer and praise to recall how magnificent our God is, how much He loves us, and what He has done for us. Are you wondering as you look at the title of this lesson, "How is worship different than praise?"

According to the website, GotQuestions.com,

> *"Praise is the joyful recounting of all God has done for us. It is closely intertwined with thanksgiving as we offer back to God appreciation for His mighty works on our behalf....Worship, however, comes from a different place within our spirits. Worship should be reserved for God alone (**Luke 4:8**). Worship is the art of losing self in the adoration of another. Praise can be a part of worship, but worship goes beyond praise. Praise is easy; worship is not. Worship gets to the heart of who we are. To truly worship God, we must let go of our self-worship. We must be willing to humble ourselves before God, surrender every part of our lives to His control, and adore Him for who He is, not just what He has done. Worship is a lifestyle, not just an occasional activity....It is through true worship that we invite the Holy Spirit to speak to us, convict us, and comfort us....Through worship, we realign our priorities with God's and acknowledge Him once more as the rightful Lord of our lives. Just as praise is intertwined with thanksgiving, worship is intertwined with surrender. Worship is an attitude of the heart."[14]*

As I read that definition, I was struck by the idea of surrender. We must surrender every part of our being to God. We must recognize that He is sovereign and surrender our wants, desires, attitudes, will, mind, and hearts to Him. In doing so, we come to the end of our selfishness and bow before Him as a servant. He can do what He wants when He wants and how He wants. He is over all, in all, and through all. He is King of all kings and Lord of all lords. He is supreme. And the fact that He loves you and me as one of His very own children with an undying love demands our bended knee. It demands our loyal worship of Him. He alone is God.

As we see the beauty of God in all His glory, splendor, and wonderful works, we find the basis of our praise and the reason we worship. We will not always have the answers to why we are going through tough times. But as we learn to persevere in the midst of them, through our worship and surrender to God and His will, we will find joy and the ability to carry on.

We often equate worship with singing, and while we should worship God with song, worship is so much more. It is a lifestyle that should permeate everything we do. It is also important to note that we can praise God, but we can also praise others. We praise people for jobs well done, for promotions, for being elected to an office, and for making the team. We even praise the dog for learning how to sit on command. But worship—that is reserved for God alone. He is the only one worthy of worship.

DAY 1
— READ *NEHEMIAH 12:27-30* —

As we look at the idea of worship, we will focus on how we need to prepare our hearts and minds to be in the intimate presence of God. We will look at attitudes we need to adopt and areas of our life that we need to surrender and give to Him. Today we will focus on developing a pure heart.

1 According to **Nehemiah 12:27**, how are the priests and people to celebrate the dedication of the wall?

_____

_____

_____

_____

According to **Nehemiah 12:30**, what do the priests do?.

_____

_____

_____

_____

2 In the Old Testament, God established that sin must be covered by the shedding of blood from an innocent sacrifice. But the sacrifice of an animal on the temple altar was only a temporary sin covering. Countless sacrifices were offered to cover countless sins, over and over again. God promised a coming Messiah whose shed blood would be once and for all, eliminating the need for further sacrifices. This promise was fulfilled when God sent His own Son, Jesus, to be the final and perfect sacrifice who died as payment for the sins of everyone. Our need is to recognize and receive the sacrificial gift of Christ. Read **Hebrews 9:13–15** in the New Living Translation (NLT) (on the next page), and record what you learn.

"UNDER THE OLD SYSTEM, THE BLOOD OF GOATS AND BULLS AND THE ASHES OF A HEIFER COULD CLEANSE PEOPLE'S BODIES FROM CEREMONIAL IMPURITY. JUST THINK HOW MUCH MORE THE BLOOD OF CHRIST WILL PURIFY OUR CONSCIENCES FROM SINFUL DEEDS SO THAT WE CAN WORSHIP THE LIVING GOD. FOR BY THE POWER OF THE ETERNAL SPIRIT, CHRIST OFFERED HIMSELF TO GOD AS A PERFECT SACRIFICE FOR OUR SINS. THAT IS WHY HE IS THE ONE WHO MEDIATES A NEW COVENANT BETWEEN GOD AND PEOPLE SO THAT ALL WHO ARE CALLED CAN RECEIVE THE ETERNAL INHERITANCE GOD HAS PROMISED THEM. FOR CHRIST DIED TO SET THEM FREE FROM THE PENALTY OF THE SINS THEY HAD COMMITTED UNDER THAT FIRST COVENANT."

_____
_____
_____
_____

3 The idea of being pure comes from having a life that is free from sin. What do the following verses say about purity in our lives?

Matthew 5:8

_____
_____
_____

Philippians 1:9–11

_____
_____
_____

2 Timothy 2:22

_____
_____
_____

4 How do we keep our way pure according to the following verses?

Psalm 119:9–11

_____
_____
_____

Ezekiel 20:19–20

_____

_____

_____

5 Worship begins with a pure heart. Is there anything you need to confess to God today? Have you been harboring an attitude that might be impure? Do you need to forgive someone who has wounded you?

_____

_____

_____

DAY 2
— READ *NEHEMIAH 12:31-42* —

The people were accustomed to seeing workers and watchers on the wall, but this day, they see worshipers. It is time to dedicate the work of God, the completion of the wall, to the Lord. The people are excited over the things they have been able to accomplish through God's strength. Think of the amazing perspective they must have had standing on that wall. They were able to see the large group of people it took to complete the task and the vast number of people the wall would protect. They were able to see how large the wall was. They were able to get a new view of everything the people had done and how God had used each person to complete the work. It was truly a day to celebrate.

1 In this section of Nehemiah, two choirs are gathered on the wall. According to **Nehemiah 12:31**, what are these choirs appointed to do?

_____

_____

_____

_____

2 God wants us to have an attitude of thankfulness for all He has done for us. He wants us to recognize His hand in giving us all we have. It is this posture of thanksgiving that keeps us humble in recognizing the gifts of God in our lives. What do the following verses say about either thanksgiving or humility?

Psalm 69:30–33

_____

_____

_____

_____

Psalm 100:3–5

_____

_____

_____

_____

Colossians 3:15–16

_____

_____

_____

_____

3 When we are experiencing times of trial and difficulty, we need to focus on all God has done for us and celebrate His faithfulness in giving us good gifts. List some of His greatest blessings and gifts He has given you during your life.

_____

_____

_____

_____

_____

4 What do you learn about God's gifts from the following verses?

Matthew 7:7–11

_____

_____

_____

James 1:17

_____

_____

_____

5   When we are going through challenging times, it can be good to gain a new perspective—to climb on top of the wall, if you will. As we have been reminded today of God's goodness, write a prayer below, and thank Him for all He has done for you.

_____

_____

_____

_____

_____

_____

_____

_____

_____

_____

_____

_____

DAY 3
— READ NEHEMIAH 12:43 —

1   According to **Nehemiah 12:43**, what do the people offer? What is the people's response?

_____

_____

_____

On **Day 1**, we looked at the sacrificial system God established in the Old Testament. What else do you learn about the shedding of blood as a covering for sin from the following verses?

Hebrews 9:22

_____

_____

_____

1 John 1:7

_____

_____

_____

Because of Jesus' sacrifice on the cross, we are forgiven once and for all the moment we see our need for a Savior and accept Jesus as the only way we can be saved. Once we accept Him as our Savior, our sin debt is paid. Read **John 19:1–42** and record any information that speaks to your heart regarding Jesus' sacrifice for you.

_____

_____

_____

_____

_____

_____

Jesus Christ gave His life for you, being put to death in one of the cruelest manners imaginable. Given what He has done for you, what is your response to His sacrifice? Write anything God puts on your heart, and write a prayer that expresses your gratitude for His sacrifice.

_____

_____

_____

_____

_____

_____

_____

_____

_____

DAY 4
— READ *NEHEMIAH 12:44-46* —

Today we are going to look at the idea of worshiping God in our work. Our work may be a full-time or part-time job, a volunteer position in our church or nonprofit organization, or helping out in our local schools. We also have responsibilities to care for our families, whether we are raising babies or taking care of aging parents. We help our friends when they need encouragement from time to time. A person's work or job will look different from one person to another, and all these examples are part of the work God has called us to do.

Sometimes God has big plans for us, and we find ourselves in a major project or cause for Him. More often, He calls us to be there for another person who is in need. Following God's calling can be amazing, especially when we see Him use us in immediate ways. God can also use us in many simple ways, and sometimes you may never realize what has happened. It might be as simple as holding the door for someone or saying hello to someone who has felt invisible all day. The point is that we have to be obedient to go wherever God has called us.

Sometimes God will ask us to do something easy, but other times He will take us to a place of discomfort—a place that is challenging and unfamiliar and requires our dependence on Him. It will take some sacrifice to be obedient to His calling. It will take our surrender to His plan and His calling, but the joy in obedience and the blessing our obedience brings are so sweet.

1 **Nehemiah 12:44–46** records some of the ways the Israelites were appointed to serve. Write down some of the jobs and positions you see in these verses.

_____

_____

_____

_____

_____

_____

_____

2 What are some of the ways God appoints or calls people according to the following verses?

Deuteronomy 7:6

_____

_____

_____

John 15:15–17

_____

_____

_____

1 Peter 2:9–10

_____

_____

_____

3 What should be our attitude in the work God has given us to do?

Colossians 3:17

_____

_____

_____

Colossians 3:23–24

_____

_____

_____

4 Sometimes our job or task can be overwhelming and difficult. How does God say He will strengthen us to do the work He has given us?

Isaiah 35:3–4

_____

_____

_____

_____

Isaiah 41:10

_____

_____

_____

_____

1 Peter 5:9–10

_____

_____

_____

_____

5 At times it can be difficult to go to work, your place of service, or take care of your family with an attitude of thanksgiving and cheerfulness. **Psalm 62:8** tells us to pour out our hearts before God. If you are struggling or feeling dragged down in the mundane tasks of life, write a prayer to God. Pour out all that is in your heart, and ask Him to restore your joy and give you eyes to see His calling and plan for your life.

_____

_____

_____

_____

_____

_____

_____

"Never underestimate the importance of simply being physically present in the place where God wants you. You may not be asked to perform some dramatic ministry, but simply being there is a ministry."[15]

—*Warren Wiersbe*

DAY 5

— READ NEHEMIAH 12:47 —

The last area of worship we will look at is worship through giving to God. This way of giving can take many forms such as giving our tithes and offerings, giving our time to volunteer in God's service and giving our talents to use what He has given us for His glory. Our act of giving to the Lord in worship should be done freely.

1   What do you see the Israelites doing in **Nehemiah 12:47**?

_____

_____

_____

_____

2   Skim Numbers 18, a list of the Levites' (priests') duties in the temple. If you recall, Abraham and his descendants were given the Promised Land as their inheritance from God. Each tribe except the Levites was given a specific region. The Levites were set apart to be priests and workers in the temple of God. What was the Levites' inheritance according to **Numbers 18:21–24**?

_____

_____

_____

_____

_____

According to **Numbers 18:26**, were the Levites required to tithe?

_____

_____

_____

_____

_____

3 What do the following New Testament verses say about giving?

Matthew 6:1–4

_____

_____

_____

Romans 12:13

_____

_____

_____

2 Corinthians 9:6–8

_____

_____

_____

2 Corinthians 9:11–12

_____

_____

_____

4 Worship is always a matter of the heart. God does not need our money, but He does want us to give with a cheerful and pure heart. What do you learn in **Matthew 5:23–24** that speaks to the heart?

_____

_____

_____

5 Read **Luke 6:37–38**. Using this scripture as a basis, write a prayer to God and ask Him to increase your heart for giving. Ask God to bless your efforts to surrender to His will for your life.

_____

_____

_____

_____

Concluding Thoughts

This week we witnessed an amazing celebration. All the people, priests, singers, and instrumentalists joined together in dedicated praise with thanksgiving and great shouts of joy that could be heard for miles around. They were rejoicing in gratitude for what God had done, worshiping God, and surrendering to serve Him.

Where are you this week? Are you tired and weary? Maybe you need to see things from a different perspective. We are told in **Ephesians 5:20** that we should give thanks at all times and for everything, but sometimes it is very hard to see anything to be thankful for, especially when times are challenging. Ask God to show you what to be thankful for, and ask Him to help you be thankful. And when you find the good in life again, remember to give Him the credit for it. Everything you have is a gift directly from His hand. He owns all things, He created all things, and all things are His. And He generously gives you good gifts.

How about your giving record? I am not only talking about what you put in the offering plate (however, do not neglect giving God a tithe) but how flexible and generous you are with your time. Will you get up early to spend time with Him? Are you willing to serve in some unseen capacity? Are you a slave to your schedule? **Romans 12:1** tells us that we are to present our bodies for God's service, and by doing so, it is an act of worship. Are you willing to surrender?

Additional Notes

_____

_____

_____

_____

_____

_____

_____

_____

_____

Benediction

We will all go through good times and bad times, times of joy and times of sorrow, times of ease and times of pain. When challenging seasons come, when life is painful and trouble seems to overwhelm our daily routine, we must have a plan to persevere and carry on, to move forward in strength. We need His strength, His abilities, His joy, and His sustaining presence to get through.

I hope the examples in Nehemiah have given you some practical ways to persevere. I hope you now have some practical, real-life ways to help you stand strong when the waves of life crash over you and try to knock you off your feet. As we have seen these past weeks, when life is tough . . .

- *Get on your knees.* Take your problems to God. He has the power, the strength, and the wisdom to get you through your troubling times.

- *Don't be afraid to act.* Just do the next right thing. You have asked God for His direction and guidance. Now don't be afraid to act on what He is telling you to do.

- *Make sure you know your enemy.* Satan is crafty, and he is coming against you. Know his tactics. He is a defeated foe, and Jesus is stronger than Satan. In the power of Christ, you can combat any of Satan's schemes.

- *Rest in God's love.* God loves you deeply. You are His child. No matter how difficult life gets, there is rest in the arms of your God. He longs to comfort you and demonstrate His love for you.

- *Adjust your focus.* Make sure your eyes are focused solely on God. Our perspective is warped when we are focused on ourselves.

- *Abide in God's Word.* Read His Word, and let its richness wash over you. It contains everything you need for life and godliness. Search Scripture to get to know God better and gain wisdom on how to persevere.

- *Praise God.* He is worthy of your praise.

- *Stand strong.* He gives you the strength and ability to stand in even the most trying situations.

- *Surrender to God in worship.* He is King of kings and Lord of lords. Surrender to Him and worship Him through your giving and your work.

As we complete our study of Nehemiah, please know that I am praying for you—that God will continue to teach you from His Word and give you continued strength along your journey. Below is my prayer for you.

Dear Father,

Since we have been justified by faith and have peace with God through our Lord Jesus Christ and have obtained access by faith into this grace in which we stand, we rejoice in hope of the glory of God! In our suffering, we rejoice, knowing that suffering produces endurance, that endurance produces character and character produces hope. Oh Father, may we never be put to shame, because Your love has been poured into our hearts through the Holy Spirit Who has been given to us. (from Romans 5:1-5)

Lord, whatever was written in former days was written for our instruction, that through endurance and through the encouragement of the Scriptures we might have hope. I ask that You, the God of endurance and encouragement, allow us to live in harmony with one another, in accord with Christ Jesus. May we with one voice glorify the God and Father of our Lord Jesus Christ. (from Romans 15:3-6)

Father, may we walk in a manner worthy of You, fully pleasing, bearing fruit in every good work and increasing in the knowledge of You; may we be strengthened with all power, according to Your glorious might, for all endurance and patience with joy; may we give thanks to You, Father, as You have qualified us to share in the inheritance of the saints in light. (from Colossians 1:10-12)

Finally, since we are surrounded by so great a cloud of witnesses, let us also lay aside every weight, and sin which clings so closely, and let us run with endurance the race that is set before us, looking to Your Son, Jesus, Who is the founder and perfecter of our faith. Jesus, Who for the joy that was set before Him, endured the cross, despising the shame, and is seated at the right hand of Your throne. May we always remember His sacrifice, persevering under great hostility from sinners. May we not grow weary or fainthearted. (from Hebrews 12:1-3)

In the precious and holy name of Jesus Christ,

Amen

Notes

1.   Warren Weirsbe, *Be Determined* (Amersham, UK: Scripture Press Publications, 1992) 18.

2.   Warren W. Wiersbe, *Be Determined: Standing Firm in the Face of Opposition* (Colorado Springs, CO: David C. Cook, 1992), 22.

3.   "Quotes by Alan Redpath," Grace Quotes, accessed April 23, 2022, https://gracequotes.org/author-quote/alan-redpath/.

4.   "Ridicule." *Merriam-Webster.com Dictionary*, Merriam-Webster, https://www.merriam-webster.com/dictionary/ridicule. Accessed 10 May. 2022.

5.   Alan Redpath, *Victorious Christian Living* (Grand Rapids, MI: Revell Company, 1958), 118-119.

6.   Rick Warren, *The Purpose Driven Life: What on Earth Am I Here For?* (Grand Rapids, MI: Zondervan, 2012), 149.

7.   John MacArthur, *The MacArthur New Testament Commentary: 1 Corinthians* (Chicago: Moody Bible Institute, 1984), 291.

8.   Everett F. Harrison (Ed.), *Wycliffe Dictionary of Theology* (Peabody, MA: Hendrickson Publishers Marketing, 1960), 135.

9.   Timothy Keller, @timkellerncy. May 10, 2019, at 9:14 am

10.   Warren W. Wiersbe, *Be Determined: Nehemiah* (Colorado Springs, CO: Cook Communications Ministries, 2004), 119.

11.   Warren W. Wiersbe, *Be Determined (Nehemiah): Standing Firm in the Face of Opposition* (Colorado Springs, CO: David C. Cook, 2004), 149.

12.   Warren W. Wiersbe, *The Wiersbe Study Bible* (Minneapolis, MN: Thomas Nelson, 1982).

13.   "Winston S. Churchill Quotes," Goodreads, accessed April 23, 2022, https://www.goodreads.com/quotes/857718-we-make-a-living-by-what-we-get-but-we.

14.   "What Is the Difference between Praise and Worship?" Got Questions, accessed April 23, 2022, https://www.gotquestions.org/difference-praise-worship.html.

15.   Warren W. Wiersbe, *Be Determined (Nehemiah): Standing Firm in the Face of Opposition* (Colorado Springs, CO: David C. Cook, 2004), 130.

CPSIA information can be obtained
at www.ICGtesting.com
Printed in the USA
LVHW051554161222
735289LV00008B/1530